Oriental Orthodox-Roman Catholic
Interchurch Marriages
and
Other Pastoral Relationships

Oriental Orthodox-Roman Catholic Interchurch Marriages

and Other Pastoral Relationships

National Conference of Catholic Bishops
Standing Conference of Oriental Orthodox Churches

The Oriental Orthodox-Roman Catholic Consultation in the United States, which functions under the auspices of the Standing Conference of Oriental Orthodox Churches and the National Conference of Catholic Bishops, has authorized the publication of this volume. Its purpose is to make more widely known the pastoral implications of the relationship that now exists between the two communions. The book was produced under the direction of an editorial committee composed of Reverend Garabed Kochakian (Armenian Orthodox), Very Reverend Chorepiscopus John Meno (Syrian Orthodox), and Reverend Ronald G. Roberson, CSP (Roman Catholic). It has been reviewed by Bishop Howard J. Hubbard, consultor to the NCCB Committee on Ecumenical and Interreligious Affairs and is authorized for publication by the undersigned.

Monsignor Dennis Schnurr
General Secretary
NCCB/USCC

Design: Graves Fowler, Silver Spring, Md.

ISBN 1-55586-097-4

To His Eminence Mar Athanasius Yeshue Samuel
Syrian Orthodox Archbishop of the United States and Canada
December 25, 1907 – April 16, 1995

One of the Founding Members of the Official Oriental Orthodox-
Roman Catholic Consultation in the United States of America

We also wish to remember the other members of the consultation
who have fallen asleep in the Lord:

Reverend Gabriel Abdelsayed
Reverend Thaddeus Horgan, SA
Reverend Edward J. Kilmartin, SJ
Archbishop Tiran Nersoyan

MAY THEY REST IN PEACE.

CONTRIBUTORS TO THIS VOLUME

Reverend Aelred Cody, OSB
>A monk of St. Meinrad Archabbey in St. Meinrad, Ind., and editor of *The Catholic Biblical Quarterly*.

Reverend Clarence Gallagher, SJ
>Professor of Eastern Canon Law and Rector of the Pontifical Oriental Institute in Rome.

Reverend Garabed Kochakian
>Chancellor of the Eastern Diocese of the Armenian Church in the United States, New York City.

Reverend Frederick R. McManus
>Professor *Emeritus* of Canon Law at The Catholic University of America in Washington, D.C., and editor of *The Jurist*.

Very Reverend Chorepiscopus John Meno
>Archdiocesan General Secretary and Chancellor of the Syrian Orthodox Archdiocese in the United States and Canada, and Rector of St. Mark's Cathedral in Teaneck, N.J.

Reverend Ronald G. Roberson, CSP
>Former member of the staff of the Pontifical Council for Promoting Christian Unity; presently Associate Director of the Secretariat for Ecumenical and Interreligious Affairs of the National Conference of Catholic Bishops in Washington.

TABLE OF CONTENTS

APPENDICES

Throughout the past seventeen years, the Oriental Orthodox - Roman Catholic Consultation in the United States of America has become a strong forum wherein continued dialogue between our sister communions has brought us closer together in our common witness to Christ's Holy Church. We have come to know each other better and have developed a more trusting relationship in our common efforts for unity to become the Church for which Our Lord prayed when He said, " *That they may be one as we are one.* " *(John 17:22).*

The numerous research papers and documents that have been produced from our dialogue have finally led us to the preparation of this volume that addresses *Inter-Church Marriages*; a reality that we all face today in the pluralism of America. The time has come to address this issue of inter-church marriage with open minds and hearts. We are indebted to the members of the Consultation for making this important contribution that we pray will foster even closer ties with each other.

The information which appears in this book is not only informative and educational, but as well, an asset to priests of both churches who are engaged in providing pastoral guidance to couples preparing for a Christian marriage to be blessed in the church.

We welcome this guide at a time when it is most needful and express our confidence that it will provide better guidance to both clergy and laity who are preparing for marriage and the Christian formation of family, respecting one another's faith, church and tradition.

With prayers,

Abp. K. Barsamian

Archbishop Khajag Barsamian
Primate

Secretariat for Ecumenical and Interreligious Affairs
3211 4th Street, N.E. Washington, DC 20017-1194
TEL (202) 541-3020   FAX (202) 541-3183

We are fortunate to live in an era when centuries-old misunderstandings between Catholics and Oriental Orthodox have been overcome, making possible a new relationship between us. In the United States, an Official Oriental Orthodox-Roman Catholic Consultation has been working since 1978 to deepen the bonds of communion between our two Churches. The consultation has brought to life the words that the late Armenian Catholicos Vasken I spoke to Paul VI when he visited the Vatican in 1970: "We have remembered, as in a reawakening, that we have been brothers for the past two thousand years."

The consultation has addressed a wide range of theological topics such as christology, liturgy, and ecclesiology, and also pastoral questions that directly affect the lives of our faithful in the many areas where they live side by side. We have achieved much, and have reached a point where we are able to express in a concrete way how far we have come.

This book bears testimony to the path we have traveled together. It is, in a sense, our own *Tomos Agapis*—a "Book of Love" that parallels a similar collection of documents and correspondence between Popes and Patriarchs of Constantinople that began during the pontificate of John XXIII. It not only contains studies of the relationship that exists between our two communions at the national and worldwide levels, but also offers guidelines for the benefit of clergy and faithful who are involved with mixed marriages and other pastoral questions.

I highly recommend this book to all Catholics who want to know more about our Oriental Orthodox brothers and sisters, and especially to pastors in whose ministry questions about our relationship with the Oriental Orthodox arise. It is my hope that this volume will help to make the trusting and respectful relationship that exists among the members of our joint consultation a reality in the daily lives of our faithful throughout North America.

+ Howard J. Hubbard

Howard J. Hubbard
Bishop of Albany
Catholic Co-Chairman

ܬܘܒ ܕܝܠܗ ܐܦܣܩܘܦܐ
ܘܪܝܫܟܘܡܪ̈ܐ ܕܐܬܪܐ ܐܡܪܝܩܝܐ

ARCHDIOCESE OF THE SYRIAN ORTHODOX CHURCH
IN THE UNITED STATES & CANADA

ARCHBISHOP
MAR ATHANASIUS Y. SAMUEL.
PRIMATE

April 3, 1995

49 Kipp Avenue
Lodi, N.J. 07644
201-778-0638

To the Clergy of the Archdiocese
and to all Readers of the present work

Dearly Beloved in Christ,

    May the peace and grace of our Lord Jesus Christ be with you all. The present volume has grown out of the ongoing Official Oriental Orthodox-Roman Catholic Consultation in the United States of America. For almost two decades, we have come together in the love of Christ for the fulfillment of what our Lord Himself so fervently prayed for "that they may all be one; even as Thou Father, art in Me, and I in Thee, that they also may be one in us, so that the world may believe that Thou hast sent Me (St. John 17:21)." Our conversations, though frank and open, have been in a spirit of Christian brotherhood, and we have learned much about one another and indeed about ourselves.

    The present work is the result of much prayerful effort and concern for the spiritual well-being and growth of the faithful entrusted to us by Christ. Very early on in our discussions it became clear that the pressing pastoral needs of our two families in Christ require not only our immediate concern, but also our wholehearted willingness and mutual responsibility to realize in concrete action our Christian calling of "one Lord, one faith, one baptism, one God the Father of us all, Who is above all and through all and in all (Ephesians 4:5 and 6)." We urge all the clergy of our Archdiocese to carefully study the present volume and to put into practice the guidelines offered.

    We pray that our humble efforts may be joined with the working of the Holy Spirit to restore us all to the fullness of the stature of Christ that the Holy Church may more perfectly reflect the image in which we have been created and called as children of God and brothers and sisters in our Lord.

Sincerely in Christ,

+athanasius Y. Samuel

Athanasius Y. Samuel,
Archbishop

INTRODUCTION
by Reverend Ronald G. Roberson, CSP

On October 8, 451, as many as five hundred bishops gathered in the city of Chalcedon on the Asian shore of the Bosphorus, across the water from the fabled dome of the great church of Hagia Sophia in Constantinople. The bishops had assembled to grapple with a controversy that was raging within the Christian community—a controversy that had to do with nothing less than the Church's teaching about the person of Jesus Christ. The dispute focused on the relationship between the humanity and divinity of Christ, a question which, the bishops realized, was decisive for the Church's teaching about the way in which humans can be saved.

At the fifth session, on October 22, the bishops approved a *Definition of the Faith* that set forth what would become the classical christological teaching of most Christians: that in Christ there is one person (the divine Logos) but two natures (one human and one divine). In this way the bishops hoped to articulate a formula of faith that would achieve a reconciliation between the disputing parties.[1]

Chalcedon's christological definition was supported by the Byzantine imperial government, and it was almost universally accepted within the Empire. But beyond its borders, the Chalcedonian teaching met with stiff resistance. In those areas there was a strong attachment to the earlier formula of Cyril of Alexandria, who had spoken of "the *one* incarnate nature of the Word of God." In fact, Chalcedon's formula was rejected by virtually the entire Patriarchate of Alexandria, by about half the Patriarchate of Antioch, and by the distant Churches of Armenia and Ethiopia. At the time these Churches constituted a very significant portion of the Christian world. Therefore it would be fair to say that the Council of Chalcedon did not achieve its goal of establishing unity and peace within the Church. This took place largely, some scholars have pointed out, because there had been no authentic dialogue between the disputing parties on the council floor.[2]

---

[1]   For a succinct discussion of the issues and historical circumstances of the Council of Chalcedon, see Leo Donald Davis, *The First Seven Ecumenical Councils (325-787): Their History and Theology* (Collegeville, Minn.: The Liturgical Press, 1983) 170-206.

[2]   Wilhelm DeVries, *Orient et Occident: les structures ecclésiales vues dans l'histoire des sept premiers conciles œcuméniques* (Paris: Les Editions du Cerf, 1974) 160.

The divisions that Chalcedon failed to overcome were followed by other divisions within the Christian world. Those who accepted Chalcedon would divide five centuries later into what are now the Roman Catholic and Eastern Orthodox Churches and, in the sixteenth century, the major Protestant communities would emerge from the Roman Catholic Church. Those who did not accept the Chalcedonian formula evolved into a loose communion of Churches now known as Oriental Orthodox: the Armenian, Coptic, Syrian, Ethiopian, Eritrean, and Malankara Orthodox Churches.

For the most part, the various Christian communions remained aloof from one another, frozen in the entrenched positions of the past, for many centuries. Those who rejected Chalcedon were derisively called Monophysites, while the Oriental Orthodox maintained that Chalcedon smacked of Nestorianism. Only in the twentieth century has a new outpouring of the Holy Spirit coaxed Christians to set aside the wounds of the past and seek full communion with each another again in the one Lord.

In the 1960s and 1970s, an astonishing series of developments totally changed the atmosphere between Catholics and Oriental Orthodox. The authentic dialogue that did not take place at Chalcedon finally began in earnest. First, theologians of the two communions engaged in dialogue under the auspices of the *Pro Oriente* foundation in Vienna, Austria. They tackled the age-old problems that divided them, proposed solutions, and made recommendations to their Church leaders. The work of the theologians quickly bore fruit when popes and heads of the Oriental Orthodox Churches had historic encounters in the following years. In common declarations signed on those occasions, the two sides agreed that the ancient christological division has been substantially resolved and set forth vast areas in which the two communities can cooperate in pastoral ministry. They even spelled out conditions for a certain level of sacramental sharing.

Such recommendations can be put into practice most fruitfully in areas where Oriental Orthodox and Catholics live side by side in substantial numbers. And the only country in the world where the Catholic Church exists alongside sizable communities of all the Oriental Orthodox Churches is the United States. The Catholic Church is the largest denomination in this country, and there are Armenian, Syrian, Coptic, Ethiopian, and Malankara Orthodox diocesan structures in the U.S.

This unique situation has made possible the development of a relationship between Catholics and Oriental Orthodox as a group that could not exist elsewhere. Indeed, the Official Oriental Orthodox-Roman Catholic Consultation in the United States of America, co-sponsored by the Standing

Conference of Oriental Orthodox Churches and the National Conference of Catholic Bishops, is the only formal dialogue that exists between the Catholic Church and the Oriental Orthodox Churches as a group in the world. Much of the consultation's work has been devoted to finding ways to implement in our own country the pastoral recommendations made by the leaders of our two Churches.

The present volume is a collection of studies devoted to this question, with special emphasis on the problem of mixed marriages. It begins with the two joint documents that the national consultation has produced: one on the purpose, scope, and method of the dialogue, and the other on the Eucharist. Next are pastoral guidelines on mixed marriages, one written from an Oriental Orthodox perspective (by Rev. Garabed Kochakian, Chancellor of the Eastern Diocese of the Armenian Church in America, and Very Rev. John Meno of the Syrian Orthodox Church of Antioch in the U.S.), and the other from a Roman Catholic perspective (by Professor Clarence Gallagher, SJ, Rector of the Pontifical Oriental Institute in Rome). The Catholic guidelines are complemented by a paper on marriage in the new Eastern Code of Canon Law by Rev. Frederick McManus of the Canon Law Faculty of The Catholic University in Washington, D.C. This is followed by a history of the national consultation by Rev. Aelred Cody, OSB, of St. Meinrad Archabbey, Indiana, and an overview of the contemporary relationship between the Catholic and Oriental Orthodox Churches at the international level by Rev. Ronald Roberson, CSP.

Six appendices complete the volume. They include a compendium of Common Declarations issued by Catholic and Oriental Orthodox Church leaders, a selection of other pertinent documents, an overview of the history and present situation of the Oriental Orthodox Churches, a glossary, bibliography, and directory of the Catholic and Oriental Orthodox Churches in the United States of America.

It is the hope of the consultation that this book will be used as a practical guide for members of both Churches at a time when, although still divided, we are finding new ways of working together for the good of all our faithful as we journey down the path toward the reestablishment of full communion. ~

Purpose, Scope, and Method of the Dialogue Between the Oriental Orthodox and Roman Catholic Churches (1980)

by The Official Oriental Orthodox-Roman Catholic Consultation in the United States

Introduction

The Oriental Orthodox and Roman Catholic Churches share in the same Spirit, the Incarnate Son, and the Father through saving faith. For this profound reason our Churches have much to contribute to one another from the spiritual treasures they derive from their holy traditions. The responsibility to open channels of communication which may facilitate this spiritual exchange derives from the Gospel command given to all Christians to love one another both in word and act after the example of the Father who "gave his only Son" (Jn 3:16) and Jesus Christ who "loved his own . . . to the end" (Jn 13:1). To share with one another our lives, ourselves, and our spiritual and material riches in the cause of strengthening the faith of those who are in Christ—this is the only adequate response to the one who calls us to "love one another as I have loved you" (Jn 15:12).

It is in this spirit that we begin our dialogue. We recognize that the Church is called to be the community of those who live a common life like the Trinity; a worldwide community in which no single member or local Church is foreign to any other member or local Church but rather one in which each has its measure to receive and give. Hence this dialogue aims at contributing to the establishment of the conditions that make possible the visible manifestation of the love which already exists between our Churches. The goal of the dialogue, therefore, is to work toward the realization of a mutually acceptable profession of faith, which embraces the whole range of the life of faith, and a corresponding communion of life, which respects the freedom of Christian communities in all things that do not pertain to the essentials of the life of faith.

As a step in this direction, this dialogue intends to promote (1) mutual growth of our Churches through the reciprocal sharing in doctrinal and spiritual traditions as well as liturgical life; (2) cooperation in our common responsibility for furthering the unity of all Christian Churches and preaching the Gospel to the world; and (3) unity of action between the Churches in responding to the various problems and questions that arise in the numerous Christian communities and the world at large.

In brief, since the main concern of this dialogue is the fostering of conditions that favor full communion between our Churches, it has both a practical and doctrinal orientation. It looks to ways of deepening unity in Christ through both concrete acts of love and theological discourse, for the dialogue in love which nourishes unity includes both act and word.

I. Dialogue in Love—Practice of Love

As a consequence of the estrangement between our Churches that took place many centuries ago, and the accompanying insensitivity toward the ecclesial status of one another, both Churches have attempted to proselytize individual members and particular local communities of the other Church. Such activity has been especially detrimental to the stability and growth of certain Oriental Orthodox Churches. Moreover, this practice is contrary to the demands of an ecclesial dialogue in love, which assumes that both Churches, as Churches of Jesus Christ, should live in a communion which respects the ancient traditions and styles of life of one another.

The long history of estrangement, intensified by well-meaning though at times self-serving ecclesiastical activity, must come to an end. This can be achieved only through a dialogue in love which leads us to seek new ways to remedy the effects of actions of the past which do not harmonize with the new experience of the ecclesial status of both Churches; concrete acts of love, especially when costly, demonstrate that both Churches recognize one another as true Churches of Jesus Christ deserving of the right to life, respect, and support. Therefore the daily life of the two Churches commands our attention. We intend to consider what practical means of cooperation are possible in the social, moral, and political spheres: whatever means can be employed to afford the faithful of both Churches the experience of their oneness in Christ. Beyond this the dialogue intends to respond, where possible, to the needs of other Churches, especially in lending support to heal schisms wherever they exist. Finally, it accepts the task of developing practical suggestions for ways the two Churches can effectively cooperate in common witness to the Gospel before the world.

II. Dialogue in Love—Theological Discourse

Theological dialogue is a requirement of the dialogue in love. For one of the aspects of the dialogue in love is the mutual commitment to seek the truth together so that both partners may live more fully in the truth.

This mutual commitment to seek the truth is not based on speculation concerning the possibility of arriving at knowledge of God and the mystery of the human person. It is grounded on the conviction that divine revelation of these mysteries has occurred in history, reaching its fullness in Jesus Christ; that the Holy Spirit was sent to make this revelation accessible to all people until Christ's second coming by sustaining and nourishing the Church of Jesus Christ in the truth.

The Church is the place where God's word is always present and affirmed. But it is the "tent of the word of God" and, in its proper activity, sacrament of the truth: the way which gives all people access to God. This means that the dogmas, by which the Church formulates its experience of the mystery of God acting in history, function as an introduction into the mystery of faith: God the Father revealing himself in Jesus Christ through the Spirit. The totality of the mystery cannot be expressed adequately in any of its dogmatic formulations. Dogmatic statements are historically conditioned expressions of the divine truth. Although affirming divine truth, they remain in need of continual reinterpretation so as to be made more fully intelligible in changing historical and cultural contexts. Therefore Christian theology has the task of continually re-reading dogmas in the light of Scripture and Tradition as well as the newer insights and expressions of the life of the Church. Just as in the early undivided Church, so now the written Scripture is accepted as our norm of faith in the context of the living Church, which interprets it in the light of past and present ecclesial self-understanding. Since we believe that our Churches possess the Spirit of God, we are also convinced that our mutual witness of faith in dialogue can contribute to a deeper knowledge of the divine truth.

However, this dialogue can be carried on only in the atmosphere of love. For charity furnishes the insight that the Spirit dwells in each of us and that we can only expect the other to accept the witness of faith insofar as he is convinced in faith, and this means in the Spirit. This conviction of the presence of the Spirit in the partners in dialogue, grounded on the experience of mutual love, determines the style of the dialogue. It is only properly conducted in a non-authoritarian, open, and discursive way. Since there exists in all truly Christian dialogue the presence of Christ in the Spirit, the partners should maintain an openness to receive from one another the liberating power of the Gospel and share with one another their personal understanding of the truth as the Spirit reveals it.

1. Conditions for Theological Dialogue
The word *dialogue* means a speaking together with the accent on togetherness. By its very nature, it aims at broadening areas of mutual agreement. Consequently it is imperative that the partners be open to one another (*reciprocity*) and ready to learn from one another and change ways of thinking

and acting when the truth discovered through the conversations leads in a new direction *(mutual commitment)*. In brief, dialogue aims at mutual enrichment and unity at as many levels as possible: human relations, truth, practical collaboration.

What is demanded of dialogue in general must be found in this dialogue between members of the Churches of the Oriental and Roman Catholic traditions. The partners of the dialogue should consider each other as equals. This means that (1) each should view the other as faithful to the Gospel according to his lights; (2) each should regard the other as possessing the Spirit and so capable of teaching or learning in speaking or listening through the Spirit; and (3) both partners share in common the fundamental spiritual goods which are the mutual possession of both Churches.

2. Theological Discourse and Differences between Churches

While the principle of equality between the members of the dialogue must be affirmed, the Churches which they represent have developed characteristic theological approaches to the Christian economy of salvation to which correspond differences in the organizational form of church life, liturgy, and spirituality. Many of the differences are clearly superficial, but others are more substantial. Since we reject that form of doctrinal indifferentism that claims that all positions held by the Churches of Jesus Christ have equal validity, the partners of this dialogue are committed to seeking together resolutions to those seemingly incompatible divergences in content and expression of doctrine and the variations in the concrete style of ecclesiastical life which derive from them.

In this connection, we recognize the existence of a hierarchy of truths within the diverse formulations of Christian faith. The partners of this dialogue, therefore, accept the task of articulating this hierarchy of truths and explaining the relationship between these truths as they see it. Here the problem of language inevitably arises. Since it is a question of establishing communication between two theological traditions, it is clear that the partners must submit the language they use to critical study. To avoid traveling along parallel lines wherein the same thing is meant by different words, the mutual effort must be made to discover the mentality, the genius of the culture, the philosophical outlook, traditions, and styles of life that lie behind what is being said.

3. Methodology of the Theological Dialogue

The method of the dialogue involves several elements which can operate in succession or concurrently: (1) exchange of ideas, where each one presents a point of view on the subject under discussion; (2) comparison of ideas to bring out differences and likenesses; (3) further investigation of shared posi- tions; and (4) highlighting of aspects of the subject previously unnoticed, which leads to further investigation.

Concerning the subjects of the dialogue, a distinction must be made be- tween (1) truths confessed in common; (2) truths obscured in one community but developed in the other; and (3) religious insights even in areas of divergence (e.g., particular forms of worship; emphasis on certain aspects of Christian life).

Once this distinction has been established, the following approach is recommended:

(A) Begin the dialogue with elements that unite the two Churches. This will foster a positive spirit which, it may be hoped, will prevail when dealing with areas of disagreement. Moreover, it will afford a yardstick by which the partners are in a better position to evaluate differences and make changes when necessary.

(B) Explain doctrine in a constructive way—avoiding defining by op- position, which leads to overstressing or hardening of certain positions.

(C) Aim towards a constructive synthesis of doctrine, which attempts to account for the whole scope of revealed truth.

(D) When examining theological problems between the Oriental Ortho- dox and Roman Catholic Churches, do not ignore the historical developments since the New Testament and Patristic periods, nor the current theological de- velopments and ecclesial practices in both Churches. Also keep in mind that the Spirit of the Church is both a conserving and renewing Spirit.

(E) When examining problems between the two Churches, distinguish between divergences that are compatible and those that are seemingly in- compatible with reference to full communion.

4. Themes of the Theological Dialogue

Knowledge of Christian faith comes to us in varied ways. They parallel the ways in which we reach out for and allow reality to enter our consciousness. The world is laid open to us by our moods and feelings (sentient field), by our interaction with people (interpersonal field), by the personal and social stories which serve to organize our feelings and to form a sense of continuous identity (narrative field). In these primal fields, the knowing subject is not consciously detached from the object known. However, the subject may consciously detach himself from the object to be known and seek to know the real in itself (theoretic field).

Corresponding to these ways by which knowledge of the faith is ob- tained and expressed, theologians distinguish between two types of theological statements: (1) those that derive more directly from the experience of the life of faith and are expressed in self-involving language; and (2) those that attempt to formulate in a scientific way the doctrinal content of the more direct expressions of faith. Since the liturgy, with its self-involving language, is the best expression of the ecclesial experience of the life of faith, it provides an indispensable source of the dogmatic statements of the official Church and the theological reflection of scientific theology. Thus it is fitting that this dialogue begin with the study of the liturgies of the two Churches and, in particular, with the sacraments of the Church.

Moreover, since the mystery of Christ, in which all Christian theology is grounded, is expressed and realized in the Church most perfectly through the celebration of the divine liturgy, the Eucharist, it seems most appropriate that this dialogue begin with and continually return to this theme. For the value of particular theological positions and practices of the Church can be measured by the harmony they display with the faith expressed in the celebration of the Eucharist.

In the discussions about the Eucharist, or whatever topic is singled out for analysis, the participants are resolved to adopt as a working principle the one which Pope John XXIII formulated in his opening address to the participants of Vatican Council II:

> The substance of the ancient doctrine of the *depositum fidei* is one thing; the manner in which it is presented is quite another.[1]

There already exists a concrete example of the application of this principle which has brought our Churches closer together. The joint statement published by the Syrian Orthodox Patriarch Ignatius Jacoub III and Pope Paul VI at the end of the Patriarch's visit, October 1971, reads in part:

> Pope Paul VI and Patriarch Mar Ignatius Jacoub III are in agreement that there is no difference in the faith they profess concerning the mystery of the Word of God made flesh and become really man, even if over the centuries difficulties have arisen out of different theological expressions by which this faith was expressed.[2]

---

[1]   John XXIII, Opening Address of the Second Vatican Council, October 11, 1962.
[2]   Text in *Acta Apostolicae Sedis* 63 (1971) 814-815. See also Appendix A, p. 103.

This agreement provides us with a solid basis for the hope that in "speaking the truth in love" (Eph 4:15a) this dialogue will make a contribution to our further growth together "into him who is the head, into Christ, from whom this whole body, joined and knit together by every joint with which it is supplied, when each part is working properly, makes bodily growth and upbuilds itself in love" (Eph 4:15b-16). ∼

Agreed Statement on the Eucharist (June 9, 1983)

by The Official Oriental Orthodox-Roman Catholic Consultation in the United States

(1) We agree that in the Eucharist the Church assembled is carrying out the injunction of the Lord to do what he did in the Last Supper, in commemoration of him.

(2) We agree that just as bread and wine became Christ's body and blood at the Last Supper, so do bread and wine become the body and blood of Christ when the Eucharist is celebrated by our Churches.

(3) We agree that the power of the triune God effects the change of bread and wine into the body and blood of Christ in the Eucharist. Traditionally, this has been attributed either to the Word or to the Spirit.

(4) We agree that the exercise of this divine power most properly is attributed to the Holy Spirit as source of God's action and grace in the Church. This corresponds well with the Spirit's role as life-giver, as overshadower in the incarnation, as sanctifier who sanctifies the bread and wine, become the body and blood of Christ, so that it sanctifies us when we receive it.

(5) We further agree that the consecration of the elements is effected through Christ, the risen Lord, true God and true man, who operates through the Spirit in the life of the Church. This corresponds well with Christ's role in the Last Supper.

(6) We recognize that some Fathers of the Church, such as John Chrysostom, Severus of Antioch, and Ambrose of Milan, have taught that the Eucharist is effected by the words of Christ, "This is my body . . . ; This is my blood." For when the priest pronounces these words during the anaphora, he does not do so in his own name but as representative of Christ and the Church.

But since what Christ did, once and for all, is made present now through the work of the Holy Spirit, other Fathers have held that the

Eucharist is effected when the Holy Spirit has been invoked upon the gifts of bread and wine.

(7)   We agree that in the anaphora or canon the account of institution, the anamnesis, and the epicletic prayers are all integral parts of a functional unity, and that the function of each can be properly understood only in the context of their mutual relations.   ～

Oriental Orthodox Guidelines for Marriages with Roman Catholics

by Reverend Father Garabed Kochakian and Very Reverend Chorepiscopus John Meno

Introduction

This effort has been undertaken by the Standing Conference of Oriental Orthodox Churches in the United States, which was formed in 1973 in New York for the purpose of fostering closer relations among its member sister Churches: the Armenian Orthodox, Syrian Orthodox, Ethiopian Orthodox, Coptic Orthodox Churches, as well as the Malabar (Syrian Orthodox) Church in India.

Members of the Conference are appointed directly by their diocesan jurisdictional heads. The Conference proposed the writing of these marriage guidelines with the hope that they may assist Oriental Orthodox and Roman Catholic clergymen in the pastoral counseling of interchurch couples who are contemplating marriage and the Christian formation of a family that would evolve within the diversity of their Christian traditions. The Conference strongly emphasizes that attempting to win converts is not the intention or goal when such a mixed union is blessed. Neither clergy nor laity should entertain such notions. Rather, all concerned should work together cooperatively so that the integrity of the sacrament of marriage, when liturgically celebrated, may be maintained in the development and nurturing of the Gospel message of Christ our Lord who prayed "that they may be one as we are one" (Jn 17:22).

Thus the purpose of this study is to give guidance to Oriental Orthodox priests by providing some general background regarding the sacrament of holy matrimony, as well as specific information about the canonical rules and practices of the various Oriental Orthodox Churches concerning interchurch blessings.

Differing interpretations of the sacramental nature of marriage, especially between the Oriental Orthodox and Roman Catholic communions, will be discussed in view of marriage preparation. The following document's attention will focus on specific requirements that priests must discuss in arranging marriages between Oriental Orthodox and Roman Catholic Christians.

10

Concerning the canonical regulation of the rites of marriage of both the Oriental Orthodox and Roman Catholic traditions and the proper theological and liturgical integrity of their celebration, a great disparity of practice among the clergy of both churches presently exists here in the United States. It is only by properly celebrating the rites that the full sacramental meaning of marriage is expressed and revealed.

The Oriental Orthodox Churches, which date from the apostolic era, share a communion based upon a common definition of Christ and the co-operative action of his divinity and humanity, and upon the official rejection of the teachings expressed at the Council of Chalcedon on this matter in 451 A.D. Although the Oriental Orthodox have not enjoyed full eucharistic communion with the Byzantine (Eastern Orthodox) and Roman Catholic Churches since that time because of this theological controversy, recent discussions and meetings between theologians and representatives of these Churches have produced a convergence and a high level of mutual understanding concerning early theological and Christological debates.[1] These meetings have enabled them to achieve greater appreciation for and of each other's mode of expressing the one and the same reality, i.e., that Christ is both perfect God and perfect Man, thus removing these polemics that for too long have impeded full eucharistic communion. Nonetheless, sacramentally that unity does not yet exist in its fullness.

The Meaning of Marriage

Marriage is one of the seven sacraments of the Oriental Orthodox Churches. It is directly related to the experience of being God's people and to the mystical experience of membership in the Church. This sacrament, which blesses the union of a man and a woman, begins with the partners themselves belonging to the Body of Christ, his holy Church, and their sharing in the fullness of its liturgical life of prayer. Their witness to the Orthodox faith becomes visible in their frequent reception of holy communion and other acts of faith. Therefore, it is at the divine liturgy that they can experience together their union in Christ the Lord as husband and wife forever.

It is important to note that in the early Christian Church the marriage of a couple was validated by attending the divine liturgy and partaking of the holy communion of Christ's Body and Blood together. And, finally, receiving a

---

[1] As of 1984, the Syrian Orthodox Church of Antioch and the Church of Rome by mutual agreement have allowed their faithful to receive communion in the other Church when they are unable to attend a liturgy of their own Church.

blessing from the bishop who offered a simple prayer for their life together, the marriage was blessed by the Church. The formal ritual of marriage as celebrated today by the Oriental Orthodox evolved from these early practices.

Indeed, the free consent of the couple, both then and now, was essential in order to receive the sacramental blessing. But much more than free consent was needed. The gathered body of the Church, the sharing of the Eucharist, the experience of prayer at the divine liturgy as well as the blessing of the priest—all these together re-presented Christ in the celebration of this event as "sacrament," and were important. With our Lord at the center of this event, marriage becomes truly a Christian celebration, giving birth to a union that is sanctified, blessed, and hallowed by the grace of God. The initial place of eucharistic sharing as the married couple's central experience of faith is still preserved by the Oriental Orthodox, as the couple, both communicant members of the Church, are instructed to receive the sacrament of penance separately (private confession) and then holy communion together on the Sunday preceding their marriage.

This prenuptial sharing of the Body and Blood of Christ clearly shows that marriage is not only contractual or a legal validation of the union of a man and a woman, but also a true celebration of the entire Church, i.e., the couple, the congregation of believers, and the priest(s) who are themselves all witnesses to, and celebrants of, a new life centered in the Eucharist.

Today this eucharistic tradition is confronted with many challenges. In our pluralistic society the great diversity of religious confessions makes the ideal of a marriage between Oriental Orthodox partners less a reality in the Church community. The Church now encounters the condition of a "mixed marriage," that is, a marriage between an Oriental Orthodox and a Christian from another confession. Such situations do not change the general meaning of marriage with regard to its intent, but certainly present problems when celebrating the rites of blessing in the various Oriental Orthodox traditions.

It should be understood that while mixed marriages are neither encouraged nor forbidden by the Armenian and Syrian Orthodox Churches, they are "non-existent" in the Coptic and Ethiopian Orthodox Churches. In any case, sacramental blessing by the Church granted through the person of the officiating priest can only be administered and celebrated for those who are baptized Christians. Canonically there is no separate liturgical rite or sacramental blessing for an Oriental Orthodox and a non-Christian. The Oriental Orthodox Churches do not sanction or bless such a union.

As stated, mixed marriages are those between Oriental Orthodox and persons from Christian confessions that acknowledge belief in the holy Trinity and the divinity of Jesus Christ as Lord and Savior. The celebration of the sacrament of holy crowning, as it is traditionally called, is allowed for a mixed union out of concern for the couple's well-being. They are invited to share in prayer and to affirm to the extent possible their common faith within the rite without compromise of personal or Church integrity. This practice of *oikonomia* allows both to share in the event as much as possible. It should remain clear that the acceptance and participation of a non-Oriental Orthodox Christian in the marriage rite does not imply his/her conversion, nor does it grant him/her the privilege to actively receive the other sacraments of the particular Church that sacramentally blesses the union. It is only by the sacrament of chrismation that one becomes a member of the faith community after proper catechesis before or after the marriage.

The key to the success of a mixed marriage from the day of the ceremony to the eventual formation of a Christian family and the interpersonal relationship of the couple, as well as their extended relationships with friends and family members, is their extra sensitivity to each other in the spirit of love and sacrifice. Orthodox partners should make every effort to be sensitive to the feelings, beliefs, practices, and perspectives of their spouses. It is likewise hoped that the non-Oriental Orthodox will do the same.

These are basic standards which exist in all Oriental Orthodox Churches regarding the meaning of marriage and its sanctification by the Church in the office of her priesthood and by the witness of her faithful. However, even within this unified body of ancient Churches there are differing interpretations of these basic standards.

For example, the Coptic and Ethiopian Churches require re-baptism of Protestants, or conversion to Oriental Orthodoxy of Roman Catholics and Eastern (Chalcedonian) Orthodox. Such a requirement precludes altogether the existence of mixed marriages in these Churches. The Armenian and Syrian Churches, however, never mandate conversion or practice re-baptism, provided that the baptism of the non-Oriental Orthodox has been administered with the Trinitarian formula. With regard to the latter two Churches, notwithstanding this right of choice, the non-Oriental Orthodox individual is free to practice his/her faith without restraint. In all cases, the Christian formation of children is expected to develop in the particular Church in which the marriage was blessed. No promissory document needs to be signed.

Since marriage is understood and viewed by the Church as an indissoluble sacrament, ecclesiastical dissolution of a marriage is rarely granted, and this only in extreme circumstances such as adultery, deprivation of the marital rights of either spouse, or serious and continued physical abuse of either partner. If the blessing service of a first marriage has been celebrated in the Church and a civil divorce of the married couple has been awarded, a successive marriage blessing service celebrated by the priest requires the permission of the local ordinary bishop. In the case of the Armenian and Syrian Churches, such action is taken only by the chief pontiff or local ordinary. The Coptic and Ethiopian traditions allow successive marriage (second or third) in the Church but only with the permission of their patriarch and not the local ordinary bishop. This action by the patriarch is an ecclesiastical dissolution of the marriage altogether; the individuals will be able to receive from the Church the sacramental blessing of a first marriage. Successive marriage in the Coptic and Ethiopian Churches is allowed only for widows and those who have received the aforementioned ecclesiastical dissolution.[2]

A period of penance and self examination of the parties involved, to be determined by the priest who will celebrate the sacramental blessing, is required. It is proper for the counseling clergyman to facilitate the divorced party's acknowledgment of his/her failure and human weakness in the initial marriage. Furthermore, within the liturgical rite of a successive marriage blessing, certain passages of the prayers expressly remind the couple to persevere and to seek a fruitful remarriage. In the Syrian, Coptic, and Ethiopian Orthodox Churches, the practice of the blessing of crowns and rings is not performed for the individual who is being remarried unless his or her previous marriage was simply a civil ceremony and as such was not recognized as blessed by the Church. It is suggested that such successive marriages, should they occur, be celebrated simply and without pomp and ceremony.[3]

Some of the complexities and variances of practice regarding the rites of the Oriental Orthodox raise other questions, especially in a mixed marriage situation. At this point, we shall narrow our discussions to those marriages contracted between Oriental Orthodox and Roman Catholics, and to questions pertaining to procedure, preparation of the couple, liturgical practice, and propriety in the celebration of the sacrament.

---

[2] The two terms "annulment" and "dissolution" are not synonymous. The Roman Catholic Church understands annulment to mean that the sacramentality and reality of the marriage never truly existed. But in the Oriental Orthodox perception, a previously existing marriage can be *dissolved* based upon convincing evidence.

[3] Regarding the ritual of Holy Crowning, the Syrian, Coptic, and Ethiopian rubrics require that the crowning be reserved for that individual who is receiving the sacramental blessing for the first time. However, the Armenian Orthodox practice will offer the crowning for both partners in a successive marriage. By *oikonomia*, the disparity of liturgical practice among the Oriental Orthodox in no way affects the unity of the Faith that binds these Churches together.

Oriental Orthodox–Roman Catholic Marriages

Before focusing on these particular issues, it would be useful to summarize the Roman Catholic understanding of Roman Catholic-Oriental Orthodox marriages, since Oriental Orthodox guidelines need to take this into account.

The Roman Church views the following steps leading to the blessing of a marriage as essential if church order is to be fully respected:

(1) The pastors of both parties involved should properly instruct the couple in order to avoid possible misgivings or misunderstandings before the marriage is blessed by the Church.

(2) In order to marry a Christian who belongs to another Church, the Catholic party needs to obtain the permission of his or her local bishop, technically known as a "dispensation from the impediment of mixed religion." If the marriage is to take place in an Oriental Orthodox Church, the Roman Catholic party needs an additional permission from the Catholic bishop called a "dispensation from form." Both of these permissions are needed for the sake of lawfulness or "liceity." But even if neither of them is obtained, the Catholic Church still regards such marriages celebrated in an Oriental Orthodox Church, with or without the presence of a Catholic priest, as valid. The Roman Catholic party is also asked to express his or her intention to raise any children resulting from the marriage as Catholics by assenting to the following statement: *I reaffirm my faith in Jesus Christ, and with God's help, intend to continue living that faith in the Catholic Church. I promise to do all in my power to share the faith I have received with our children by having them baptized and reared*[4] *as Catholic.*

(3) The Catholic priest with his bishop's consent may invite an Oriental Orthodox clergyman to be present at the Catholic service and offer a prayer. Alternatively, a Catholic priest may accept an invitation to offer a wedding prayer of blessing in an Oriental Orthodox church.

(4) Regardless of whether the sacramental rite is celebrated in a Roman or Orthodox sanctuary, the marriage should be recorded by both churches in their sacramental registries.

(5) In an Armenian or Syrian Orthodox church, the invited Roman Catholic priest may be fully vested in the liturgical attire required to celebrate a wedding.

(6) At a service celebrated in an Armenian or Syrian Orthodox sanctuary, the Roman Catholic priest is permitted to stand at the holy altar table at the side of the Oriental Orthodox priest who is the official celebrant.

---

[4]   That is, receiving all the other sacraments of the Catholic Church.

(7) The Roman Catholic priest who is present at the wedding service in an Armenian or Syrian Orthodox sanctuary may read from the prophecy and/or epistle from the Oriental Orthodox rites, and at the conclusion of the entire service he may offer a prayer over the couple as prescribed for weddings from the Roman Catholic Sacramentary.

It should be emphasized that the Roman Church recognizes the sacramental validity of a mixed marriage celebrated by an Oriental Orthodox clergyman. Here a question arises regarding the need to acquire a dispensation at all, since the two Churches recognize each other's sacraments as valid. Nonetheless, such a dispensation is required if the marriage is to be recognized as "licit" by the Roman Church.

It is also important to remember that the Roman Catholic priest in all weddings serves as the witness of the Church while he observes the bride and the bridegroom bestow the sacrament upon each other. The man and woman are considered to be the ministers of the sacrament of marriage. Such an understanding is not consistent with Oriental Orthodox sacramental theology in which the priest (since he is the representative of the bishop who is liturgically and canonically the chief dispenser of God's grace) is perceived as the celebrant and sole sacramental minister.

Family Faith Formation

With regard to children and the family's faith formation, when Oriental Orthodox marry within their own communion, even if they are from varying national faith-traditions, little difficulty arises between husband and wife since the children's Christian formation is ordinarily decided by mutual agreement. Problems most often arise in the case of Oriental Orthodox-Roman Catholic marriages where the couple give no or little consideration to their children's spiritual formation. The entire family faith experience suffers.

We have already discussed the role of the Church as witness in the Roman Catholic and Oriental Orthodox theologies of marriage. We now turn to the role of the laity as witnesses to the sacramental blessing of marriage, and to their participation in the ceremony itself.

The lay witnesses in the ceremony of blessing are the best man and the maid/matron of honor. In all the Oriental Orthodox Churches, the best man should be a member of the faith community.[5] This is not always the case, how-

---

[5]   Interestingly, the Coptic Orthodox Church's practice in America allows two females to augment the two male witnesses of the sacraments. Sensitive to certain prevailing circumstances, some Armenian dioceses in America allow a non-Oriental Orthodox to be best man by participating in the marriage rite as a "social witness," while at the same time placing a member of the Armenian or a sister Oriental Orthodox Church as "sacramental witness" in order to remain faithful to the discipline of the Church.

ever. In many instances, non-Orthodox have held this position of honor, without prejudice to the required norm which must prevail whenever possible.

The Best Man
In the Armenian and Syrian Orthodox tradition, the primary witness is the best man. During the ceremonies of both of these Oriental Orthodox Churches, the best man holds a cross between the couple (Syrian) or over their heads (Armenian). In the Coptic tradition each witness holds a candle during the service. In the Armenian Church the best man later serves as the baptismal godfather to the child(ren) of the couple. This is a national custom and not a theological regulation or requirement. In an Ethiopian rural tradition, the male witness serves as a marriage counselor to the couple if there are difficulties in their relationship.

The Maid/Matron of Honor
The presence of the maid/matron of honor is essential not only to satisfy the civil requirement of most American states that there be two witnesses to the marriage, but also to satisfy the ecclesial need for lay witnesses to the sacrament. In the Syrian Orthodox Church the maid/matron of honor is required to sign the marriage certificate that is issued by the Church along with the best man.

Validity of Sacrament vs. Validity of Marriage
There is no question about the validity of the sacrament of marriage when it is celebrated and blessed in an Oriental Orthodox sanctuary with an Orthodox priest officiating, provided that the partners and their respective witnesses are in compliance with church regulations.

However, when an Oriental Orthodox-Roman Catholic couple is united in holy matrimony in a Roman Catholic ceremony, certain questions arise for the Oriental Orthodox concerning its full sacramental validity.

The sacramentality of the service is not in question if an Oriental Orthodox priest is present at the ceremony and offers prayers blessing the union of the couple at an appropriate point during the service (see Appendix A and B for text of suggested prayers). His presence and active participation satisfies the requirement of the Armenian and Syrian Orthodox Churches that a form of sacramental blessing be bestowed.

However, if no Oriental Orthodox bishop or priest is present at such a Roman Catholic ceremony to give his blessing to the couple, the sacramental grace bestowed upon them remains unclear. The marriage is valid. But the

Oriental Orthodox still have a question about the sacramentality of the marriage as described above because a marriage as celebrated according to the Latin rite, where the couple bestows the sacrament upon one another, does not fully correspond to our theological understanding of sacraments and their administration. Therefore, if no Oriental Orthodox clergy is present to bless the couple at a Roman Catholic ceremony, the sacramentality of the marriage appears to be deficient in view of Oriental Orthodox form, theology, and practice, according to which all sacraments are seen as grace bestowed through the officiating priest. (For an example of this posture of the Church, see Appendix B, *The Armenian Prayer of Crowning*, and footnote 8.)

Promise Made, Promise Fulfilled
If the two Churches fully recognize the integrity of the sacramental theology and sacramental validity of the other, then for the Oriental Orthodox it appears unnecessary, ambiguous, and even improper to require promises concerning family Christian formation and development. Certainly an inquiry should be made regarding the couple's faith intentions and commitments. If there is a sincere and committed acknowledgment of faith, it seems to the Oriental Orthodox that requiring a promise before granting permission to celebrate a particular Orthodox rite of blessing is perhaps too demanding, if not unnecessary. The liceity of form versus validity of sacrament seems to confuse the issues here.

The basic question centers on a living Christian faith commitment by both parties—not on a promise to one tradition or another, but on a promise to God and to their future offspring.

**Suggested Procedures for Oriental Orthodox Clergy
in Marriage Preparation**
(1) The Oriental Orthodox priest should inquire of the Roman Catholic party if he/she intends to remain a communicant member of the Roman Church. If the answer is yes, then it behooves the Oriental Orthodox priest to inform the party that he or she should obtain permission from the local Catholic bishop to marry a non-Catholic and, if appropriate, to marry in an Oriental Orthodox ceremony. In this way the Catholic will be acting with the full approval of his or her Church.

(2) If the Roman Catholic party intends to remain within the fold of his/her Church then he/she should meet with his/her pastor to understand and fulfill the requirements of the Catholic Church. This may even call for additional prenuptial instruction.

(3) The pastors of both parties should be in contact with each other as the marriage plans and instructional process move ahead to avoid any misgivings or misunderstandings concerning the obligations of the parties.

(4) A copy of the dispensation(s) granted by the Roman Church should be given to the Oriental Orthodox priest who will be celebrating the sacramental blessing. This duplicate will be filed in the marriage registry of the Oriental Orthodox parish.

(5) A copy of the baptismal and confirmation (chrismation in the case of Eastern Catholics) certificate from the Catholic Church must be presented to the Oriental Orthodox priest.

(6) The Oriental Orthodox pastor should ask the Catholic party if this is the first marriage. Should there be a civil divorce from a previous spouse, copies of the documents verifying the divorce decree must be acquired and submitted to the Oriental Orthodox ordinary for review and acceptance in order to obtain permission to celebrate a successive marriage. For the Catholic party, it may also be necessary to obtain an annulment of the first marriage from the local Roman Catholic marriage tribunal before this can take place.

If an ecclesiastical annulment has been officially granted by the Catholic Church to the Catholic party, further documentation for remarriage is not required.

Should there be questions that are not satisfactorily answered by the Roman Catholic parish priest, the Oriental Orthodox-Roman Catholic couple may inquire at the local Catholic diocesan chancery for further clarification regarding the proprieties of mixed marriages.

N.B. *The above guidelines do not pertain to the Coptic and Ethiopian Churches, because mixed marriages do not exist in these two Oriental Orthodox traditions.*

Conclusion

It is our hope that these guidelines will be useful to both Oriental Orthodox and Roman Catholic priests who are preparing mixed couples for the sacrament of marriage. As the couple focuses on the common aspects of their Christian faith and tradition that they shall share as husband and wife rather than the issues that divide them, the clergyman will be able at least to provide them with the basic foundation of a spiritually healthy and meaningful Christ-centered relationship. The decision and choice to live out the faith within the tradition in which their union was sacramentally blessed is an important consideration, particularly in regard to family faith formation. Though eucharistic unity between Roman Catholics and Oriental Orthodox is not presently a reality, this in no way minimizes the respect that should be extended toward each other's Church, nor does it deny that they share a similar Christian faith. Nonetheless, affirming a commitment from the couple to practice and live out their faith is the major objective of the priest who shall bless the holy union not only on behalf of this man and woman whom he unites and crowns into marriage, but likewise for the sake of their posterity. ∼

APPENDIX A

From the Order of Solemnization of the Sacrament of Matrimony According to the Ancient Rite of the Syrian Orthodox Church

Here the priest shall join their right hands together saying:
O our beloved children, we have a custom received from our Fathers to admonish you and make you diligent. Know that you are standing in the presence of God, Who examines the hearts and the innermost, and in front of the holy altar, the cross, the adorable Gospel and in the presence of this gathering. From this time we entrust you each to each other (and pronounce you man and wife).[6] God Himself will surely be between you and me. I am innocent of your faults. Behold, O our son, this is your wife whose hand we have placed in yours, and whom we have entrusted to God and to you. Hold her diligently. Remember that you have to answer for her in the presence of God on the day of judgment.

APPENDIX B

The Canon of the Rite of Holy Matrimony: The Prayer of Crowning According to the Armenian Apostolic Orthodox Church

Blessed are You O Lord God, the only beneficent and mighty one who created heaven and earth and every creature therein.

You also created man in Your image and made him lord and sovereign over all of Your creatures. We now pray to You O Lord; bless [the Crowns of] Your servants (N. & N.) into marriage, as You had blessed [the crowns of] the righteous ones. For You have invited these servants for Your blessing [and have placed a crown of precious gems upon their heads.][7]

You, O Lord, blessed the wedding in Cana of Galilee and showed Your divine glory to Your disciples by changing the water into wine. You did not

---

6   This phrase has been added to the Syriac original.
7   The bracketed references to crowning are to be deleted in a mixed marriage, since the crowning within the normative context of the Armenian rite will not take place.

despite marriage but rather *as a high priest blessed it and established it by your own action when you said, "Them that God has joined together let no one separate."*[8]

O Holy One who lives in Your Saints, keep the wedlock of these Your servants holy, and unite them under the yoke of Your dispensation in the spirit of meekness, loving one another with modest behavior, pure in spirit, without giving cause for shame, without impudence and always ready to do good works, so that departing from the temptation of the Evil One, they may be preserved in health of soul and body, under the protection of Your angels and with the sign of Your Triumphant Cross.

Therefore O Lord Our God with Your mercy protect these Your servants all the days of their lives. Plant them as a fruitful olive tree in the House of God, so that living in righteousness, in purity, and godliness, in accordance with Your good will, they may see the children of their children who may become a people of God and glorify Your holy name, and bless the All-Holy Trinity, the Father, and the Son and the Holy Spirit, now and forever and unto the ages of ages. +Amen.

APPENDIX C

The Prayer of the Joining of the Hands
According to the Armenian Apostolic Orthodox Church

Here the priest shall join their right hands together saying:

The Greeting and Exhortation:
See my dear children in Christ (N. & N.), according to the Divine Command and the laws of the holy fathers of the Church, you have come to this holy church in order to be lawfully [crowned and] wedded into holy matrimony. May God keep you in mutual love, lead you to a ripe old age, and make you worthy of the incorruptible crown in heaven. But observe that in this world there are various trials and tribulations and other kinds of afflictions. Yet it is the command of God that you both must help each other and remain faithful to each other from this day forward, for better, for worse, for richer for poorer, in sickness and in health until death parts you.[9]

---

[8]   The words "blessed it and established it by your own action when you declared, Them that God has joined together let no one separate" signify the actual action of the priest who is "representing" Christ bestowing the sacramental grace and the establishment of marriage upon the couple.

[9]   The bracketed references to crowning are to be deleted in a mixed marriage because the crowning within the normative context of the Armenian rite will not take place.

21

The Joining of Hands:

God took the hand of Eve and gave it into the right hand of Adam, and Adam said: This is bone of my bone, flesh of my flesh. She shall be called woman for she was taken out of man. Therefore, shall a man leave his father and mother and shall cleave unto his wife and they shall be one flesh. Wherefore, them that God has joined together let no man separate.

+ The Benediction:

May God be in the midst of these his servants and may they not be shaken; may God help these his servants from morning until morning. Amen.

APPENDIX D

Marriage in the Ethiopian Tewahedo Church[10]

Arrangement and Engagement of Marriage

According to the established principle of the Church, the male must be at least eighteen years of age and the female fifteen years of age. After the two voluntarily agree, consent of the parents of each party is also required. When approved by both parents, then the engagement of the couple can be arranged by church officials, the two parties, male and female, the parents of each and the spiritual father of each party whether or not the parents and their children are members of the Ethiopian Church. The spiritual father together with the parents of the children will witness and sign a testimony to verify their devotion to the Ethiopian Orthodox Church. In addition, the Church official will inquire of the couple of their willingness to marry and of the parents concerning their approval. The couple will then go to a bishop or archimandrite. However, if neither official is available, they will go to a priest. Then the clergyman will read the Gospel concerning the marriage and explain its importance to the couple, after which they will sign in the special book designated for marriage. Finally, the clergyman will say a special prayer and benediction. After this they shall receive the certificate of engagement that states that they are eligible for marriage.

The Performance of the Marriage

Eight days before the performance of the marriage ceremony, in order to notify the Church, the couple must go to the church where the marriage is to be

---

[10]   The following is taken from Archbishop Yesehaq, *The Ethiopian Tewahedo Church: An Integrally African Church* (New York: Vantage Press, 1989).

performed and submit the certificate to the head of the Church. On the day of the marriage ceremony, the bridegroom and bride, together with their parents, the spiritual fathers, and their respective relatives, will go to the church very early on Sunday morning. According to the Church rite, the clergy will perform the sacrament of holy matrimony and the divine liturgy, at which time the newlyweds will receive communion.

The matrimonial service is conducted as follows:

(1) The bridegroom and his party enter the church by the northern door. Then the bride and her party enter by the southern door.

(2) The bride and the bridegroom sit on the southwestern side of the church, where a place has been specially prepared for them.

(3) They shall lay their hands together on the Gospel and the cross while making the following solemn vow: *In life, time of difficulty, in sickness, and under other similar circumstances we will help, comfort, and encourage each other, until death do us part. For this, God is our witness.*

(4) The husband and the wife are then robed in brightly colored church vestments.

(5) A ring is placed on the ring finger.

(6) They are both crowned and anointed with holy oil.

(7) Then they receive communion.

The following symbols used in the matrimonial service have great meaning:

(1) The robe signifies the sonship and daughtership with God and symbolizes the happiness and glory they will inherit in heaven.

(2) The rings signify the faith or religion.

(3) The cross signifies the temptation the couple will encounter in life because of their commitment to the faith.

(4) The crowns symbolize the honor they will inherit in heaven.

(5) The holy oil signifies the gift of the Holy Spirit.

For those Christians who follow such matrimonial principles, their children will be blessed, as it is written in the Scripture: *the generations of the upright will be blessed, and also wealth and riches shall be in the house and his righteousness endureth forever* (Ps 112:2-3).

Concerning Those Who Have Been Married Outside the Church

In the case of those who have been married outside the Church, their spiritual fathers should teach them and convince them to obey the principles of marriage set forth by the Church and to receive communion. Those who refuse repentance and the advice of the priests shall be denounced publicly by the priest.

Conditions Under Which a Second Marriage is Performed

Second marriage is performed as follows:

(1) He/she finds a previously unmarried person of good repute or a widow of good repute.

(2) The couple should come to an agreement and go with their spiritual fathers to the Church official to obtain permission (as previously mentioned).

(3) After saying the solemn agreement, they then sign the book of engagement and receive the certificate of engagement.

(4) The couple then go to the church, where the priest must pray for them the Absolution of the Son as well as the Prayer of Penitence. Then they receive communion and become man and wife.

If one of them is a young man or woman who has never been married before, the sacrament of matrimony is performed especially for that person in the morning. At the end of the service, exhortation is given by the priest and they are advised to observe that in this world there are various trials and tribulations, such as sickness and poverty and other kinds of affliction and that they must help each other and remain faithful to each other.

Divorce

The Church does not accept divorce except for reasons of adultery, but if either of them dies, then the other can marry, unless he or she wants to remain single.

"A wife," says St. Paul, " is bound to her husband as long as he lives. If the husband dies, she is free to be married to whom she wishes, only in the Lord" (1 Cor 7:39).

If any person married under the principles of the Church desires separation or divorce, the problem is investigated to determine which individual is at fault. The matter will be evaluated according to the canon law of the Church. Whoever is guilty will be corrected through penance, and the marriage will once again be restored. However, if the guilty party will not repent, he or she will receive judgment as pronounced in the canon law of the Church.

We are aware of the fact that every married person has his/her unique problems that lead to separation and divorce. If the couple do not have confidence in each other, if they allow themselves to live in an atmosphere created through assumption and imagination, then their total lives are vanity, disgrace, and poison for their children. They are husband and wife in name only. It would have been better for them to remain single than to live a miserable life. Nevertheless, if an effort is made, such problems can be controlled through patience, trust, and understanding.

APPENDIX E

Egyptian Islamic Law and Christian Law

The marriage requirements in this guideline for the Ethiopian Orthodox Church in practice are similar to those of the Coptic Church of Egypt.

In order to protect the Christian union of the couple from being subject to Islamic law, which attempts to suppress the Christian faith that is expressed and lived by the couple, though they are both Orthodox, and at the same time undermines the integrity of Christian marriage, the Coptic Orthodox Church's *registration practice* expects the non-Copt to register as an Egyptian Copt, or the Copt to become a member of the non-Coptic community (i.e., Armenian, Syrian, or Ethiopian Orthodox). Such a practice of registration will protect the member of a sister Oriental Orthodox Church from being subject to Islamic law.

Regarding liturgical and sacramental interaction between members of the sister communions, there would be no prohibition in terms of active and mutual participation in the life of the Church.

Mixed Marriages Between Catholics and Oriental Orthodox: A Canonical Guide for Catholics

by Reverend Clarence Gallagher, SJ

What are the main points that a Catholic priest should bear in mind when he is dealing with a mixed marriage—or more specifically, a marriage between a Catholic and a member of one of the Oriental Orthodox Churches? Explanation of the following three topics[1] will provide guidance for Catholic priests concerning mixed marriages with the Oriental Orthodox:

(1) The importance of the agreement in Christian faith that exists between the two Churches.

(2) The meaning of Christian marriage as set forth in the canon law of the Catholic Church.

(3) The specific legislation on mixed marriages in the Latin and Eastern Codes.

1. Agreement in Christian Faith

The first thing that should be discussed with a couple that has decided to enter a mixed marriage is the agreement in faith that unites the two Churches. The recognition of this common acceptance of faith in Christ and in his Church and sacraments underlies the new approach toward mixed marriages between Catholics and Oriental Orthodox found in both the canons of the revised Codes and in the latest edition of *The Ecumenical Directory*. We now realize more clearly that, despite important doctrinal differences that exist between the Churches, a basic unity of faith in Christ binds these Churches together—a common profession of faith in the mystery of the Incarnate Word, the Church, and the sacraments.

This agreement in faith between the Catholic and Oriental Orthodox Churches makes possible and even encourages closer pastoral cooperation between the Churches, including the mutual admission of the faithful to the

---

[1] These topics are considered specifically from the standpoint of the legislation contained in the *Code of Canons of the Eastern Catholic Churches* (CCEO) that was promulgated by Pope John Paul II in 1990. This legislation, however, does not differ in any significant way from the 1983 Latin *Code of Canon Law* (CIC). References to the corresponding Latin canons are included when appropriate.

reception of the sacraments in certain special circumstances when there is grave spiritual need. Therefore, this mutual faith in the mystery of Christ and his Church and in the sacraments should be explained clearly and carefully discussed with a couple contemplating a mixed marriage. To prepare for this discussion, priests should study the Second Vatican Council's *Decree on Ecumenism,* along with the joint declarations made in recent years by the Catholic Church and some Oriental Orthodox Churches.

2. The Meaning of Christian Marriage

In the context of this shared faith in Christ and common vision of what it means to be a Christian, the priest should examine with the couple the nature of Christian marriage. This teaching, clearly set forth in a number of documents of the Catholic Church, has been embodied in its revised law. Canon 776 of the *Code of Canons of the Eastern Catholic Churches* (CCEO) should be studied in detail (see also the 1983 Latin Code of Canon Law [CIC] canon 1055):

> The matrimonial covenant, established by the Creator and ordered by his laws, by which a man and a woman, by an irrevocable personal consent, establish between themselves a partnership of the whole of life, is by its nature ordered towards the good of the spouses and the generation and education of the offspring.

This canon is drawn directly from the Pastoral Constitution on the Church in the Modern World, *Gaudium et spes,* of the Second Vatican Council. In actual fact, this pastoral constitution, in numbers 47 to 52, provides the clearest and most authoritative statement by the Catholic Church on the nature and meaning of Christian marriage. A careful study of this teaching is an excellent introduction to the discussion of the canonical legislation on mixed marriages. Canon 776, §1 provides a clear description of the nature of Christian marriage: an irrevocable personal covenant between a man and a woman, by which they enter into a partnership for the whole of life which is geared toward the good of the couple and the generation and education of children. This formulation constitutes an important modification of previous legislation, which concentrated on the generation of children to the neglect of the essential importance of the good of the spouses.

Together with the canons on the nature of marriage, the precise nature of matrimonial consent should be considered. Exactly what is a couple consenting to in entering Christian marriage? In other words, what is the object of matrimonial consent? This is clearly stated in canon 817 of the Eastern Code (see also CIC canon 1096):

> Matrimonial consent is an act of the will by which a man and a woman, through an irrevocable covenant, mutually give and accept *each other* in order to establish marriage.

The importance of this mutual self-giving and acceptance of the other cannot be stressed enough. Without it there is no marriage. Marriage is not simply a contract in which there is a mutual exchange of gifts or promises. It is a mutual self-donation and acceptance with a view to constituting that "partnership of the whole of life" that is so beautifully described in *Gaudium et Spes* and encapsulated in canon 776 of the Eastern Code.

The couple must also consider the constituent qualities of marriage and its essential properties. These are clearly set forth in the canons. The aim of Christian marriage is twofold: the good of the couple and the procreation and education of children. The essential properties of marriage are unity (between one man and one woman) and indissolubility. The Catholic Church teaches that if one or the other of these essential aims or properties of marriage is positively excluded by either of the parties, the matrimonial consent is so seriously defective that no marriage takes place: the matrimonial ceremony is considered null and void. If such an exclusion can be proved before a Church tribunal, the Church will issue a declaration of nullity, and the parties will not be considered bound by any matrimonial bond.

It is useful to clarify the distinction between a declaration of nullity and a dissolution of a valid sacramental bond. The Catholic Church teaches that in marriage, a valid, sacramental, and consummated union is absolutely indissoluble. Moreover, since the Catholic Church considers all valid marriages between Christians to be sacramental, it considers all such marriages to be indissoluble, whether they are Catholic or not. This teaching applies, of course, only to marriages that are truly valid marriages. If, however, there are convincing grounds in a particular case for thinking that a diriment impediment existed (consanguinity, impotence, previous bond of marriage, etc.) or that the matrimonial consent was defective in a substantial way, then in fact no real marriage took place, despite all appearances to the contrary. It is in these circumstances that the Church tribunal will issue a declaration of nullity and the parties concerned will be free to contract a truly valid marriage. The Catholic Church never dissolves a valid and consummated sacramental marriage. But in cases of non-sacramental marriages in which one or both of the parties is not baptized, there are situations when the Catholic Church can and does dissolve marriages. The "Pauline Privilege," when both parties were unbaptized according to 1 Corinthians 7:12-16, is an example of such a dissolution. Another example is dissolving a marriage for the "Privilege of the Faith," by extension to a marriage where only one party is unbaptized, since it is still not a sacramental marriage.

On the sacredness and indissolubility of the matrimonial bond, there is general agreement between the Catholic Church and the Oriental Orthodox Churches. All accept Christ's injunction: "What God has joined together, let no one put asunder." However, in the interpretation of this teaching there are serious differences of view. While proclaiming the general rule on the sacredness and indissolubility of sacramental marriage, the Oriental Orthodox admit exceptions in certain circumstances when a civil divorce of a valid sacramentally celebrated marriage has been granted. It may be possible, after due examination of the case, for the Church to grant permission to remarry. This the Catholic Church does not accept. Moreover, it is also part of the Catholic Church's teaching that no human power may dissolve a valid and consummated marriage between Christians. However, many of the grounds upon which civil divorce is recognized by Oriental Orthodox authorities would in fact be considered grounds for a declaration of nullity by the Catholic Church. Overall, when a mixed marriage is proposed between a Catholic and a civilly divorced member of one of the Oriental Orthodox Churches, the matter should be referred to the Catholic Church's tribunal for careful examination.

3. Specific Legislation on Mixed Marriages in Catholic Canon Law[2]
The following canonical form must be observed in all Catholic marriages. According to canon 828 of the Eastern Code (see also CIC canon 1108):

---

[2] Fr. McManus's chapter, "Marriage in the Canons of the Eastern Catholic Churches," discusses in some detail the canons on mixed marriages that are found in the *Code of Canons of the Eastern Churches*. He explains the need for "permission from the competent authority" in each case and the conditions to be observed in granting such permission (CCEO canons 813-814). There is no matrimonial impediment involved, so it is inaccurate to talk about "dispensations" in such cases. It is a question of obtaining permission from the competent authority. But if a mixed marriage were celebrated without such permission, the marriage would not on that account be invalid. Fr. McManus has carefully described the nature of the "promises" that the Catholic party to a mixed marriage must make, in accordance with canon 814. He discusses the interpretation of this canon with particular reference to the revised edition of the *Ecumenical Directory*, especially numbers 150-152. This legislation and the relevant ecumenical directives concerning the promises are, of course, of central importance in any practical approach to a mixed marriage between Catholics and Oriental Orthodox.

> Only those marriages are valid which are celebrated with a
> sacred rite, in the presence of the local hierarch, the local
> pastor, or a priest who has received from either of these the
> faculty to bless the marriage, and at least two witnesses.

From this canon it is clear that, for a valid marriage in the Catholic Church, three things are required:

(1) For Eastern Catholics, there must be a sacred ceremony of blessing by a priest. For Latin Catholics, a deacon may perform the service, and in some cases a civil marriage is acceptable with the proper dispensation.

(2) This priest must be the local hierarch or the local pastor (or a priest delegated by either the hierarch or the pastor).

(3) There must be at least two witnesses.

This general canonical legislation, which governs marriages in the Catholic Church, is binding for all Catholics who have been baptized in the Catholic Church, whether they consider themselves to be members of that Church or not. In the Latin Code of Canon Law there is an exception clause for those who have left the Church "by a formal act" (canon 1124), but this clause does not apply to those baptized in one of the Eastern Catholic Churches. So the omission of any of these three requisites would, in ordinary circumstances, render the marriage invalid in the eyes of the Catholic Church.

However, circumstances can arise when it is not possible for this canon to be observed. For example, when a couple is in danger of death or in other exceptional circumstances (cf. CCEO canon 832 and CIC canon 1116) and it is impossible to have a priest with the required competence, a marriage celebrated before two witnesses is considered by the Catholic Church both lawful and valid. This would be a case where the natural right to marry takes precedence over normal canonical legislation. Moreover, if such a marriage takes place between two baptized persons, it is considered fully a sacrament by the Catholic Church, even if there is no priestly blessing. This follows from the Catholic Church's teaching that, in a marriage between two Christians, one cannot separate the matrimonial contract from the sacrament.

There is another exception to the general rule concerning canonical form which deals directly with mixed marriages between Catholics and Oriental Orthodox. This exception is clearly stated in canon 834, §2 of the *Code of Canons of the Eastern Churches* (see also CIC canon 1127, §1):

> If the Catholic party belonging to an Eastern *sui iuris*
> Church celebrates marriage with a member of an Eastern

> non-Catholic Church, the form of marriage prescribed by
> law is necessary for lawfulness; for validity, however, a
> priestly blessing is required, presuming that all is observed
> in accordance with the law.

This canon is of primary importance. It was introduced by the Second Vatican Council for ecumenical reasons to avoid having large numbers of invalid marriages and to protect the sacrament. (For further reference, see the Vatican Council's *Decree on the Eastern Catholic Churches*, number 18, and the discussions that surrounded this change in Catholic legislation.) What does this canon mean in practice? It means that if a Catholic, even without permission or dispensation from the competent authority, were to go ahead and marry an Oriental Orthodox Christian in that person's Church, with the blessing of the priest, then this marriage would be considered valid and sacramental in the eyes of the Catholic Church. In other words, all mixed marriages between Catholics and Oriental Orthodox that are celebrated with a priestly blessing are considered valid sacramental marriages by the Catholic Church.

However, for such a marriage to be considered lawful by the Catholic Church, the Catholic party must obtain a dispensation from the law requiring canonical form from the competent authority. In the case of Latin Catholics, the competent authority is the local Catholic bishop. However, this is not the case for Eastern Catholics. Canon 835 of the Eastern Code states:

> The dispensation from the form of matrimonial celebration prescribed by law is reserved to the Apostolic See, or
> to the patriarch, who should not grant it except for a most
> serious reason.

This canon is peculiar to the Eastern Code; such a reservation is not found in the Latin Code of Canon Law. For the Eastern Catholic Churches, the dispensation from form is reserved to the Apostolic See or the patriarch, who is instructed by the canon to grant it only for "a most serious reason." If an Eastern Catholic marries an Oriental Orthodox Christian in an Oriental Orthodox Church, that marriage is considered perfectly valid and sacramental. If, however, the Eastern Catholic party wishes to have a valid and *lawful* marriage, application must be made to the Apostolic See in each case, or to the patriarch, in order to obtain a dispensation from the law that requires such marriages to be blessed by his/her own Catholic parish priest (or delegated priest). Moreover, the patriarch may grant such a dispensation only for "a most serious reason." A number of Eastern Catholic bishops have protested against this reservation of their power to dispense. Indeed, it is difficult to harmonize such a reservation with the ecumenical tenor of the revised legislation on mixed marriages. On the one hand, the Catholic Church recognizes the validity of all mixed marriages celebrated in Oriental Orthodox Churches and blessed by their priests. On the other hand, it says that permission should not be granted for such marriages to take place except for the most serious of reasons!

Nor can the reservation be defended by referring to the supreme importance of the "sacred rite" for Eastern Christians. The sacred rite is not in dispute here. It is presupposed in the hypothesis that the sacred blessing by an Oriental Orthodox or other Eastern priest will take place. Canon 834, §2 of the Eastern Code distinguishes between the "form prescribed by law" (which is required for lawfulness) and the sacred rite which is always required for validity. It is the dispensation from the *forma a iure praescripta* that is reserved. Some authors maintain that since the law binds only "for lawfulness" and not under the pain of invalidity, the local bishop of the Eastern Catholic party can grant the necessary dispensation. This is certainly a common-sense solution, but the authors provide no authority for such an interpretation of canon 835 of the Eastern Code. So the problem remains. In the United States, some of these difficulties have been mitigated by granting the faculty to dispense in such cases to the Apostolic Nuncio in Washington, D.C.

One last point concerns the requirement of at least two witnesses. Canon law says nothing concerning the sex—or even the religion—of the witnesses. Normally, of course, the witnesses will be members of the Catholic Church for a Catholic wedding. However, circumstances may indicate that the witnesses, or one of the witnesses, may belong to another Christian Church. Local custom, too, will play a part in choosing witnesses. In this matter the law leaves the couple freedom of choice, provided, of course, that the witnesses are capable of the juridical act of witnessing a marriage both in civil and in canon law.

One final word of advice. A priest helping a couple prepare for a mixed marriage should inform himself fully about the particular law of the Orthodox Church to which the non-Catholic party belongs. Each Oriental Orthodox Church has its own legislation concerning mixed marriages, and some Churches simply refuse to permit them.

4. The Kerala Agreement—A Model for Legislation in Practice

The Catholic Church and the Malankara Syrian Orthodox Church in India reached an agreement on mixed marriages in November 1993. The agreement received the approval of the supreme authority of each of the Churches and was published on January 25, 1994. It is an example of how the legislation we have been considering may be put into practice. The agreement is based on the common faith declaration that was made by Pope John Paul II and the Syrian Patriarch of Antioch, Ignatius Zakka I Iwas in June 1984. Given this shared faith in the mystery of the Church and the sacraments, the Pope of Rome and the Syrian Orthodox Patriarch accepted the possibility of closer pastoral cooperation that would include reciprocal admission to the sacraments of penance, the Eucharist, and anointing of the sick in exceptional circumstances and when serious spiritual need existed.

The text of the agreement is very brief, but it clarifies the common understanding of the sacrament of matrimony shared by the two Churches:

> Man and woman created in the image of God (Gen 1:26-27) are called to become sharers of the eternal divine communion. The sacrament of marriage is an image of this divine communion. Marital intimacy and self-effacing sharing are reflections of the deepest interpersonal sharing within the Trinitarian communion.

In this theological context, the Catholic Church and the Syrian Orthodox Church in India have approached the question of mixed marriages and have specified areas of agreement. The Churches agree that the sacrament of matrimony "is divinely confirmed by Christ with the seal of unity and indissolubility, and ordered towards the good of the spouses and the generation and education of offspring. . . . Our two Churches accept the sacredness and indissolubility of the sacramental bond of marriage and consider the conjugal relationship as an expression of the above communion [i.e., between Christ and his Church] and a means to achieve self-effacing mutual love and freedom from selfishness which was the cause of the fall of humanity."

The agreement goes on to make the following important statement concerning mixed marriages:

> Our two Churches desire to foster marriages within the same ecclesial communion and consider this the norm. However, we have to accept the pastoral reality that interchurch marriages do take place. When such occasions arise, both Churches should facilitate the celebration of the sacrament of matrimony in either Church, allowing

the bride/bridegroom the right and freedom to retain his/ her own ecclesial communion, by providing necessary information and documents. On the occasion of these celebrations, the couple as well as their family members belonging to these two Churches are allowed to participate in the holy Eucharist in the Church where the sacrament of matrimony is celebrated. We consider it also the great responsibility of the parents to pay special attention to impart to the extent possible and in mutual accord proper ecclesial formation to their children in full harmony with the tradition of the ecclesial communion to which they have to belong.

The full text of the agreement, along with the pastoral guidelines issued by the respective Churches for their members, is included in this volume. The agreement is epoch-making and constitutes an extremely important milestone in the ecumenical dialogue between the Churches that openly claim to be "sister Churches." A profound mutual respect between the Churches—and a compassionate understanding toward the conscience of the parties who wish to marry—is evident throughout the agreement. The following statements from the agreement show this deep spirit of mutual understanding:

> . . . that both Churches should facilitate the celebration of the sacrament of matrimony *in either Church.*

> . . . allowing the bride/bridegroom the *right and freedom to retain his/her own ecclesial communion.*

> . . . the couple as well as their family members belonging to these two Churches are allowed to participate in the holy Eucharist *in the Church where the sacrament of matrimony is celebrated.*

These examples constitute some of the most practical expressions yet seen of the mutual respect and understanding between sister Churches that should characterize the whole ecumenical dialogue. The agreement takes seriously the fact that mixed marriages can and often do take place between two committed Christians who are deeply attached to their respective

Churches, and the fact that these two Christians share the same faith concerning a basic belief in the mystery of the Incarnate Word and his Church and sacraments. The 1994 Kerala Agreement on Mixed Marriages is a great step forward in the journey toward Christian unity.

The same respect and understanding are found in the *Pastoral Guidelines on Marriage between Members of the Catholic Church and of the Malankara Syrian Orthodox Church* that were promulgated by the Catholic Church, along with the text of the agreement. These are perfectly clear and straightforward. They embody the main points of the agreement and add clarifying norms in three areas: (1) the preparation of interchurch marriages; (2) the celebration of interchurch marriages; and (3) the pastoral care of Catholic-Syrian Orthodox interchurch families.

The Catholic priest helping a couple prepare for a mixed marriage should familiarize himself thoroughly with these guidelines and explain them to the couple. On the whole, the guidelines are clear and self-explanatory; a few require further explanation.

Note that it is the bride/bridegroom who should select the Church in which the marriage is to be celebrated (no. 12), and "written permission" from the respective bishops is required (no. 13). "The liturgical minister should be the parish priest of the Church where the marriage is celebrated, or his delegate from the same ecclesial communion" (no. 17). The general prohibition of the joint celebration of mixed marriages by both ministers is repeated here:

> There is to be no joint celebration of marriage by ministers of both Churches. The marriage may be blessed by the Catholic or by the Syrian Orthodox minister. However, there could be some kind of participation at the liturgical service by the other minister who could read a scriptural passage or give a sermon (no. 18).

This prohibition is in harmony with the general law of the Catholic Church (cf. CCEO canon 839; CIC canon 1127) and avoids any confusion over who in fact presides over the ceremony. The permission for the couple and their families to jointly share in the holy Eucharist is another important point, which springs directly from a shared belief in the holy Eucharist.

Of particular ecumenical importance is pastoral guideline number 21:

> The Catholic partner is to be reminded that he/she has to commit him/herself to imparting to their children proper

> Catholic formation, *to the extent possible and in agreement with his/her partner* (cf. *Ecumenical Directory* numbers 150-152). Such formation should be fully in harmony with the Catholic tradition to which he/she belongs.

This guideline reflects a deeply ecumenical spirit. It constitutes a particular interpretation of canon 814 of the Eastern Code and is also a practical application of the Second Vatican Council's teaching on freedom of conscience (cf. *Dignitatis humanae*, no. 2). The reference to the *Ecumenical Directory*, nos. 150-152, helps clarify what is intended by the phrase, "to the extent possible and in agreement with his/her partner." It calls for special study.[3] The directive displays an openness of mind towards Orthodox Christians and presupposes a mutual understanding of the ecclesial nature of each Church which was unheard of not so many years ago. This understanding is a practical consequence of the mutual faith shared by the Catholic Church and the Eastern Churches not in full communion with the Catholic Church. It follows logically from the fact that, in accordance with the teachings of the Second Vatican Council, we find in these Churches "true sacraments, and above all, by apostolic succession, the priesthood and the Eucharist, whereby they are still joined to us in closest intimacy" (*Unitatis redintegratio*, no. 15).

Pastoral guideline number 21 is based on a profound respect for the Christian faith of the non-Catholic Christian. It is a practical recognition of the obligation concerning the education of the children that the non-Catholic partner may feel "because of his/her own Christian commitment." Even if the non-Catholic partner explicitly refuses to allow the children to be baptized and educated in the Catholic Church, this does not necessarily imply that the local hierarch must refuse permission for the mixed marriage in question. This is an innovation that will surprise a number of commentators on the recently revised canon law on mixed marriages. However, it seems to be clear from the *Ecumenical Directory*:

> In order to judge the existence or otherwise of a "just and reasonable cause" with regard to granting permission for this mixed marriage, the local Ordinary will take account, among other things, of an explicit refusal on the part of the non-Catholic party (*Ecumenical Directory*, no. 150).

---

[3] For a more detailed look at this guideline, see Fr. McManus's article, "Marriage in the Canons of the Eastern Catholic Churches."

Pastoral guideline number 24, which states that "any declaration of the nullity of such marriages is only to be considered with the consent of the bishops concerned from both Churches," could cause some difficulty. Either a marriage is valid or it is not, and if there are serious grounds for considering a particular marriage to be null, then the parties have the right to ask a Church tribunal to examine the marriage. It is not clear, therefore, how the consent of the respective bishops relates to this guideline. However, the pastoral guideline has probably been introduced to ensure that procedures concerning nullity and/or divorce should be considered jointly by both Churches.

Again, the Kerala Agreement on Mixed Marriages represents an important step forward in the ecumenical dialogue. We look forward to seeing how this agreement is put into practice and also whether it will affect the ecumenical dialogue with other Eastern Churches, which presently do not permit mixed marriages and insist that either the Catholic party become Orthodox or the Orthodox party become a Catholic. ∼

Marriage in the Canons of the Eastern Catholic Churches[1]

by Reverend Frederick R. McManus

T his selective review of the present norms or laws for the celebration of the sacrament of marriage in the several autonomous Eastern Catholic Churches[2] has been prepared primarily to inform Christians of the Oriental Orthodox Churches. The review, it is hoped, will contribute to the ecumenical dialogue of the Catholic Church with those ancient Churches.[3] It is important to remember, however, that the canonical dimensions and demands for the holy sacrament of Christian marriage are far less important than the sacrament itself, the doctrinal and theological bases for the canon law on marriage, and the pastoral ministry of both ordained and lay Christians in assistance to and support of the wives, husbands, and children of Christian families. Preoccupation with canonical questions should in no way minimize what is more important. The canon law is at the service of the Christian people.

1. Nature of the 1990 Collection of Canons

Pope John Paul II, Bishop of Rome, promulgated the Code of Canons of the Eastern (Catholic) Churches, called the *Codex Canonum Ecclesiarum Orientalium*, on October 18, 1990. On October 1, 1991, the feast of the Protection of the Blessed Virgin Mary, the code or collection became effective general or common canon law for those autonomous or *sui iuris* Eastern Churches that are within the full communion of the Catholic Church, and specifically in full com-

---

[1] This paper also appeared in *The Jurist* 54 (1994): 56-80. The original text has been adapted for this volume.

[2] Eastern Catholic Churches are in full communion with the Church of Rome and with the other Churches that are in full communion with that See. These Churches, about twenty in number, are called *sui iuris*, meaning semi-autonomous or relatively autonomous. For a valuable compendium of information on these Churches, and on the other Churches "of the East" not within the full Roman Catholic communion, see Ronald G. Roberson, *The Eastern Christian Churches: A Brief Survey*, revised 3rd edition (Rome: Pontifical Oriental Institute, 1990).

[3] A more extensive—but again rather brief—review was prepared by Clarence Gallagher, "Marriage in the Revised Canon Law for the Eastern Catholic Churches," *Studia Canonica* 24 (1990): 69-90. For a canon-by-canon commentary in English, readers are referred to Victor J. Poshpishil, *Eastern Catholic Marriage Law According to the Code of Canons of the Eastern Churches* (Brooklyn: St. Maron Publications, 1990). No additional references will be given below to this substantive commentary, but it should be consulted for an initial appraisal and interpretation of the canons on marriage in the Code of Canons of the Eastern Churches.

38

munion with the Roman See. The papal document of promulgation, called an apostolic constitution, is entitled *Sacri Canones,* from its opening words.[4]

Before a review of some of the canons concerned with marriage in this new body of church law, the Catholic understanding of the code must be explained: It emanates from Pope John Paul as the bishop of the Church of Rome founded by the mission, witness, and martyrdom of the Apostles Peter and Paul. In accord with his ancient title, Vicar of St. Peter, and as the first bishop and head of the college of bishops, the present pope gave this code of canons to the Eastern Catholic Churches.

In other words, it was not in his role and office as Roman or Western patriarch that Pope John Paul decreed this body of canon law, but rather as the chief bishop of the Catholic Church. It goes without saying that this office of the pope as head of the whole college of bishops and as chief lawmaker of the holy Catholic Church is not readily appreciated, much less accepted, by the Churches with which we are not in full communion.

The enactment of this 1990 code of canons might have been carried out better synodically, that is, by the Roman bishop together with the patriarchs and other hierarchs of the affected Eastern Catholic Churches. Or, the Eastern Catholic patriarchs and other hierarchs themselves might have assembled synodically and then given the new law to their own Churches without papal intervention. The right of these particular Eastern Catholic Churches and of all the "non-Latin" or Eastern Churches to govern themselves had already been formally acknowledged by the Second Vatican Council[5] and by the author of the new code, John Paul II.[6]

---

[4]   The official Latin text of the code, together with an unofficial English translation prepared by the Canon Law Society of America and approved by the bishops of the Eastern Catholic Churches in the United States, appears in *Code of Canons of the Eastern Churches: Latin-English Edition* (Washington: CLSA, 1992). The volume also contains an English version of the papal constitution. This translation will be used throughout this chapter.

[5]   Decree on Ecumenism *Unitatis redintegratio,* November 21, 1964, no. 16; Decree on the Eastern Catholic Churches *Orientalium Ecclesiarum,* November 21, 1964, no. 5. It is worth adding that the Eastern Catholic hierarchs participated fully in the deliberations and decisions of the Second Vatican Council, under the influence and movement of the Holy Spirit, often with an impact greater than their numbers in the assembly.

[6]   This acknowledgment is found, among other places, in the apostolic constitution *Sacri Canones.* Self-governance is recognized not only for particular or individual Churches, such as the local Churches of a single disciplinary and ritual patrimony, but also for groups of such particular Churches. This may explain the mention, in the second paragraph of *Sacri Canones,* of the discipline decreed by the seventh-century Quinisext (Panthekti) Synod in Trullo. On the one hand, the constitution recognizes the Trullan law for those Churches which took part in that council; on the other hand, it does not affirm that all the canons of Trullo oblige the Latin Church or, for that matter, the Armenian Apostolic Church, for example, or other Oriental Orthodox Churches.

At the same time, in recognition of the general principle of ecclesial conciliarity, the preparation and development of the 1990 collection of canons were carried out with exhaustive consultation and deliberation involving both hierarchs and canonists of the Eastern Catholic Churches. This was done in two lengthy stages of the process, from 1927 to 1957 and from 1972 to 1990.

Significantly, the initial inspiration of the Eastern code in the late 1920s was the pastorally successful Code of Canon Law of the Latin (or Western Catholic) Church issued in 1917.[7] Moreover, the Eastern code was directly and greatly influenced, in perhaps half of its 1,546 canons, by the 1983 revised Code of Canon Law of the Latin Church. Such large-scale derivation or dependence may be explained in part by the influence, for better or worse, of Latin church legislation and church order upon the Eastern Catholic Churches in recent centuries; it also reflects in part what was thought, rightly or wrongly, to be necessary or useful church law derived from the Latin Church's experience.

Nonetheless, it was the clear mandate and explicit intention of the redactors who prepared the new code of 1990 that the Eastern canonical traditions—expressive of different theologies and church order and diverse ritual and cultural patrimonies—should be respected and embodied in the canons. More important, this was the explicit intention of Pope John Paul II, who is to be understood as the formal legislative authority. The good faith and intent of the undertaking to preserve the Eastern tradition were expressed by the pope himself: "We judge that this code [of the Eastern Catholic Churches] is to be considered in the highest degree as derived from the ancient law of the Eastern Churches."[8]

Still more important, however, especially for ecumenical endeavors undertaken in common with the Oriental Orthodox Churches and other Churches following ancient Eastern traditions, is the underlying principle

---

[7] Some hesitations are expressed at times about the usage "Latin Church" (*Ecclesia latina*), but it is an understandable terminology regularly used in all Roman canonical documents. It refers to the Roman or Western patriarchate, to which, for an example, the 1983 Code of Canon Law was directed by Pope John Paul II. The Roman or Latin Church usage—followed by the Second Vatican Council as well—is to use "Catholic Church" to embrace both the several autonomous Eastern Catholic Churches and the Latin Church. A common alternative used in many countries is "Roman Catholic Church." Understandably the latter term, which is not used in papal or curial documents, is not fully acceptable to Eastern Catholics (whether Byzantine or Armenian, Maronite or Melkite), unless it clearly and exclusively refers to the reality of the full communion of their Churches with the Roman See.

[8] *Sacri Canones.*

enunciated by the Second Vatican Council of 1962-1965. The 1964 conciliar decree on the Eastern Catholic Churches, called *Orientalium Ecclesiarum*, states emphatically that its disciplinary norms (and thus equally the norms of the later Eastern code of canons) were to be seen as "dispositions established for the present conditions until the Catholic Church and the separated Eastern Churches come together in the fullness of communion."[9] This point is echoed in the already mentioned apostolic constitution *Sacri Canones*.[10] Current disciplinary norms (the new code) are indeed firm and stable in the present circumstances of the Eastern Catholic Churches. Yet they may be considered almost as provisional and transitory and certainly subject to all needed change, should there be, in the Providence of God and by the movement of the Holy Spirit, a restoration of the full communion of the Churches of God.

Much more could be said about the Code of Canons of the Eastern (Catholic) Churches in general, but what follows is limited to the canons on the holy sacrament of marriage, numbered 776-866. These 91 canons constitute Chapter VII of Title XVI of the code; this is the title or section on "Divine Worship and Especially the Sacraments." The very number of the canons suggests how selective and even cursory the following treatment must be.

2. The Meaning of the Sacrament

An overall examination of the new canons on marriage, even the foundational ones, may seem to reflect the (perhaps excessive) Western Catholic tradition with its concern for sharply defined formalities and for the contractual nature of the covenant entered upon by those who marry in Christ with the blessing of the Church. This may be partially explained by the juridic nature of any legal or canonical codification and by the preoccupation to determine and protect the reality, genuineness, and validity of the holy sacrament. This juridic dimension, not equally realized in other Christian traditions, is very much in the canonical tradition of the Latin Church and has influenced the Eastern Catholic Churches, as the new code itself demonstrates.

---

[9]   No. 31.

[10]   The language, both the official Latin and the literal translation into English, may appear to be convoluted, but the same point is made by the pope: "Thus it happens that it is necessary that the canons of the Code of the Eastern Catholic Churches have the same firmness as the laws of the Code of Canon Law of the Latin Church; that is, that they be in force until abrogated or changed by the supreme authority of the Church for a just cause, of which causes full communion of all the Eastern Churches with the Catholic Church is indeed the most serious, besides being especially in accord with the desire of Our Savior Jesus Christ himself."

On the other hand—and vastly more central and significant—the basic canon on marriage has the greater breadth intended by the Second Vatican Council:

> The matrimonial covenant [*foedus*], established by the Creator and ordered by his laws, by which a man and woman by an irrevocable personal consent establish between themselves a partnership of the whole of life [*totius vitae consortium*], is by its nature ordered toward the good of the spouses and the generation and education of the offspring (canon 776, §1).[11]

The paragraph reflects a recovery of the biblical concept of the marriage covenant; it is foundational in its derivation and in its placement at the head of the canons. It stands over and against other canons, which may stress more the contractual dimension of the holy sacrament, perhaps especially in the canons on matrimonial consent.[12] The covenantal and contractual concepts are not necessarily contradictory, and it must be remembered that the canons are an attempt to redact juridically what may be better expressed biblically, theologically, and ritually.

Less happily perhaps, the canon omits any reference to the action of the Holy Spirit of God in the sacrament of Christian marriage. The text would have been the richer, but the omission may be explained again by a desire for a formally juridical redaction, certainly not by any failure to recognize the power of the Holy Spirit that transforms the mutual pledges of the Christian spouses.[13]

---

[11] The language of this text reflects the teaching of the Second Vatican Council in several documents: the Dogmatic Constitution on the Church *Lumen gentium,* November 21, 1964, nos. 11, 41; Decree on the Apostolate of the Laity *Apostolicam actuositatem,* November 18, 1965, no. 11; and especially the Pastoral Constitution on the Church in the Modern World *Gaudium et spes,* December 7, 1965, no. 48. The latter places stress on the "intimate community [*communitas*] of married life and love . . . rooted in the conjugal covenant, irrevocable personal consent." The entirety of no. 48 of *Gaudium et spes* and indeed the whole chapter in which it appears (nos. 47-52) should be examined as the principal conciliar statement on marriage and on Christian marriage.

[12] Article V, canons 817-827. Canon 817, §1, however, mirrors canon 776, §1: "Matrimonial consent is an act of the will by which a man and a woman, through an irrevocable covenant [*foedus*], mutually give and accept each other in order to establish marriage [*ad constituendum matrimonium*]."

[13] In another context, the Eastern code treats the customary usage of the Spirit-filled community in language much superior to that of the Latin Church's code: "The custom of the Christian community, insofar as it responds to the action of the Holy Spirit in the ecclesial body, can have the force of law" (canon 1506, §1). This explanation of customary law has no parallel in the Latin code.

3. Marriage as Sacrament, Marriage as Contract

In accord with Western rather than Eastern tradition on marriage, the new code insists upon an identification of the marriage contract (better understood and expressed in terms of a covenant or *foedus*) with the Christian sacrament whenever Christians marry validly. This is formally stated in canon 776, §2:

> From the institution of Christ a valid marriage between baptized persons *is by that very fact a sacrament,* by which the spouses, in the image of an indefectible union of Christ with the Church, are united by God and, as it were, consecrated and strengthened by sacramental grace.[14]

Despite the richness of this formulation (although again there is no mention of the Holy Spirit), a conclusion must be drawn that Eastern canonical and theological traditions may not readily appreciate. In sharp terms, equating every authentic marriage covenant of the baptized with the holy sacrament is an affirmation that there is no authentic or genuine marriage of baptized persons without its also being a sacrament. In effect this means that for the Eastern Catholic Churches, as for the Latin Church, there is no simple way to distinguish a natural, human, civil marriage between two baptized persons from the sacrament of matrimony. The consequence, as noted below, is that certain marriages, most exceptionally, are considered valid and truly sacramental even without the priestly blessing. Likewise this canon excludes the possibility of a genuine marriage of Christians in the period prior to their receiving the priestly blessing.

The background for this position is only partially found in the teaching on the "minister" of the sacrament of Christian marriage, to be taken up next. As formulated, it is partially a modern development. To quote a succinct explanation:

> The identification of contract with sacrament was prompted in part by the attempts of certain European civil govern-

---

[14] Emphasis added. In the Latin Church's code, the matter is put more bluntly. After affirming in §1 of canon 1055 that "this [matrimonial] covenant between baptized persons has been raised by Christ the Lord to the dignity of a sacrament," the second paragraph of the canon adds: "For this reason a matrimonial contract cannot validly exist between baptized persons unless it is also a sacrament by that fact." The (unofficial) translation of the canons of the Latin code to be followed in this chapter is that prepared by the Canon Law Society of America and approved by the National Conference of Catholic Bishops: *Code of Canon Law: Latin-English Edition* (Washington. CLSA, 1983).

ments [in modern times] to gain absolute authority over marriage. The [Catholic] Church wished to avoid any semblance of a belief that the sacrament was added to the marriage contract as a kind of pious superstructure with marriage remaining essentially a secular affair. The canonical development of this question culminated in canon 1012, §2, of the 1917 code [of the Latin Church].[15]

Concretely, this means that the Catholic Church judges as sacramental all the marriages of a baptized woman and a baptized man, whether these are celebrated within its full communion (and in conformity with the canonical norms for validity) or in other Christian Churches and ecclesial communities. This may create on occasion a difficult situation in that a marriage judged fully real and valid by one Church but not yet sacramental (i.e., without the action of the Holy Spirit through the ministry of the priest and with his blessing) might be judged to be sacramental within the Catholic communion and thus subject to its norms on indissolubility. In other words, the very notion of a valid marriage of Christian people without its being counted as a Christian, sacramental marriage is foreign to the canons of both Eastern Catholic and Latin Catholic Churches.

4. The Minister of Marriage
Western theological tradition, considered "theologically certain" although not a matter of Catholic faith, holds the spouses to be the ministers of the holy sacrament, each one to the other. The canonically authorized priest is called formally the *assistens matrimonio*,[16] even though he does indeed utter the priestly blessing and regularly preside at the eucharistic celebration and sharing, by which Christian marriage is sealed and completed in accord with ancient traditions.

---

[15] Thomas P. Doyle, "Title VII: Marriage," in *The Code of Canon Law: A Text and Commentary* ed. by James A. Coriden et al. (New York: Paulist Press, 1985), 741. The canon in question is identical with canon 1055, §2, of the 1983 Latin code, quoted above in footnote 13.

[16] The function is very narrowly defined in canon 1108, §2, of the Latin code: "The one assisting at a marriage is understood to be only that person who, present at the ceremony, asks for the contractants' manifestation of consent and receives it in the name of the Church." The Latin code fails notably to demand or mention the blessing or sacred rite in this context of the canonical form of the sacrament. The definition of the *assistens matrimonio* does not appear in the Eastern code. The conventional usage, at least in some English-speaking countries, is to refer to the assisting priest (or, in the Latin Church, deacon), the *assistens matrimonio*, as the "official witness," but the usage is unnuanced and perhaps confusing.

This common, almost universal, teaching of the Latin Church concerning the ministers of marriage is the underpinning of many of the Latin Church's canons on holy marriage, although—perhaps strangely—those canons do not say directly that the spouses are the ministers of the sacrament.

Equally well known is that this teaching is not the theological tradition of the Eastern Churches. How, then, is the matter resolved in the new code of the Eastern Catholic Churches, a code in many ways dependent on the Latin code?

Canon 828, the basic canon on what is called "the form for the celebration," should be quoted in full:

> §1. Only those marriages are valid which are celebrated with a sacred rite, in the presence of the local hierarch, local pastor, or a priest who has been given the faculty of blessing the marriage by either of them, and at least two witnesses, according, however, to the prescriptions of the following canons, with due regard for the exceptions mentioned in canons 832 and 834, §2.
>
> §2. That rite which is considered a sacred rite is the intervention of a priest assisting and blessing.[17]

There is no reason to enter into the specifics demanded by other canons for valid (true, genuine, real, authentic) marriage or to stress the Latin Church's influence in the expression which refers to the priest "assisting" as well as blessing. Similarly, the phrasing of the whole canon is clearly juridical in style and purpose, with no explicit advertence to the divine action, the action of the Holy Spirit through the ministry of the priest. A major effort has been made, however, to respect the Eastern understanding: on the one hand, demanding the priestly blessing "for validity"[18] and on the other hand, not introducing the Western theology of the spouses as ministers of the sacrament.[19]

---

[17] More literally: "This rite is considered sacred by [or by the fact of or by reason of the very intervention of] a priest assisting and blessing."

[18] On the deeper respect for the Eastern teaching on the priestly ministry and blessing, see Frederick R. McManus, "The Ministers of the Sacrament of Marriage in the Western Tradition," *Studia Canonica* 20 (1986): 85-104, esp. 95-96. The Latin Church itself has greatly strengthened, in the Roman and other Latin rites, the role of the priestly blessing of marriage, along with the proclamation of the word and of course the eucharistic liturgy which is the culmination of the rite of marriage (ibid., 89-90).

[19] Canon 834, §2, gives further emphasis to the priestly blessing by requiring, in the marriages of a Catholic and a Christian of an Eastern Church not in the Catholic communion, that the requisite "Catholic" form of celebration be observed only for lawfulness. For such cases it adds: "for validity, however, the blessing of a priest [i.e., not necessarily of the Catholic communion] is required. . . ."

All this may be taken as a deliberate intent to respect Eastern canonical and even theological tradition. Nonetheless, there is a serious exception mentioned in §1 of the canon just quoted, made explicit in canon 832:

> §1. If one cannot have present or have access to a priest who is competent according to the norm of law without grave inconvenience, those intending to celebrate a true marriage can validly and licitly [lawfully] celebrate it before witnesses alone:
>   1° in danger of death;
>   2° outside the danger of death, as long as it is prudently foreseen that such circumstances will continue for a month. . . . [20]
> §3. If a marriage was celebrated in the presence only of witnesses, the spouses shall not neglect to receive the blessing of the marriage from a priest as soon as possible.

Although this canon clearly recognizes the possibility of a Christian, sacramental marriage without the priestly blessing in extreme and exceptional circumstances—in evident imitation of Latin church law—it avoids any explicit canonical (or doctrinal) definition of spouses as ministers of the sacrament. The inclusion of §3, without a parallel in the Latin code, is an evident effort to respect Eastern tradition even in this exceptional case of sacramental marriage in the absence of a priest. Finally, while this canon, together with the identification of sacrament and natural covenant, may result in complex questions of validity and sacramentality of individual marriages, it does represent some reserve or balance compared with the canons of the Latin Church.

Moreover, the new Eastern code does not introduce two other elements of the marriage discipline of the Latin Church. The first is that deacons are not recognized as canonically or sacramentally assisting at marriage or blessing marriage, something that has become a commonplace of Latin church life in recent years.[21] Second, an innovation in the 1983 Latin code

---

[20] This exceptional case, a sacramental marriage in the absence of a priest, is the same as that found in the Latin Church's law, canon 1116, §1.

[21] A number of canons of the 1983 code of the Latin Church recognize the office of deacon, at least in the absence of a priest, as regularly including assistance at marriage: 1108, §1; 1111, §1; 1112, §1; 1116, §2; 1121, §1. This enlarged office of the order of deacons in the Latin Church is immediately derived from *Lumen gentium*, Vatican II's Dogmatic Constitution on the Church, where "to assist at and bless marriage in the name of the Church" is listed as a diaconal function (no. 29).

which permits lay persons, in most exceptional circumstances, to assist at marriage does not appear in the Eastern canons.[22] These two omissions acknowledge the very different Eastern church order and its traditions.

5. "Mixed Marriages"

a. Permission for Mixed Marriages. Although the norm of canon 813—which requires the "prior permission of the competent authority" for the marriage of a Catholic and a baptized Christian of a Church not in full Catholic communion—may seem burdensome and, to some, even offensive, there is another way to view it. The so-called just cause for this permission (canon 814) is ordinarily not difficult to find. In actual practice, the competent Catholic authorities—local bishops and other hierarchs—have readily enough acted upon such requests, certainly in the United States. And this norm, however important for church order and for the good of the Christian faithful, is not an obstacle to the validity or sacramentality of the marriage of two baptized persons.

Nevertheless another aspect must be candidly appraised as burdensome and problematic. It is the canonical demand placed upon the Catholic spouse preparing for a Christian but "mixed" marriage in relation to the Christian upbringing of the children of the marriage. The matter is dealt with in canon 814 in terms of conditions placed upon the local hierarch before he grants the permission mentioned in the preceding paragraph:

> For a just reason the local hierarch can grant permission [for a Catholic to marry a Christian not in full Catholic communion]; however he is not to grant it unless the following conditions are fulfilled:
>
> 1° the Catholic party declares that he or she is prepared to remove dangers of falling away from the faith and make a sincere promise to do all in his or her power [*omnia pro viribus*] to have all the offspring baptized and educated in the Catholic Church;
>
> 2° the other party is to be informed at an appropriate time of these promises which the Catholic party has to make, so that it is clear that the other party is truly aware of the promise and obligation of the Catholic party;

---

[22] Canon 1112, §1, of the Latin code, not applicable to the Eastern Catholic Churches, reads: "With the prior favorable opinion of the conference of bishops and after permission of the Holy [Roman] See has been obtained, the diocesan bishop can delegate lay persons to assist at marriages where priests or [*precisely,* and] deacons are lacking." Nothing of this sort is contemplated in the Eastern code.

3° both parties are to be instructed on the essential ends and properties of marriage, which are not to be excluded by either spouse.[23]

Before considering the central and perhaps critical issue of the promises, long called *cautiones* in Latin canonical usage, it is important to insert two comments:

First, the canon is in substance the discipline of the Latin Church. It represents a somewhat liberalized discipline over that which governed Latin Catholics in this century prior to 1966.[24]

Second, the form or style of these promises and the like are left to the particular law of the several Eastern Catholic Churches. This is an instance of the intent of Pope John Paul II that, while the Eastern code reflects a common discipline of these Churches, they are to determine many matters by particular law.[25] This is evident in the text of canon 815:

> The particular law of each Church *sui iuris* is to establish the manner in which these declarations or promises, which are always required, are to be made, what proof of them there should be in the external forum and how they are to be brought to the attention of the non-Catholic party.[26]

b. Nature of the Promises. What can be said to help understand the promise or promises required of those subject to the Eastern code (and to the Latin code as well)? Clearly, the promises (no. 1 of canon 814) are not among the "essential ends and properties" of Christian marriage (no. 3 of the same canon). Moreover, the making or taking of the promises is by no means en-

---

[23] Aside from the requirement of "just and reasonable cause" in the corresponding Latin Church canon 1125, only the slightest verbal changes (for improved Latinity) were made when this canon was introduced into the new Eastern code. For an explanation of the canon, as it appears in the Latin code, see the commentary by Doyle, cited in footnote 15 above, 802-804.

[24] It may be of interest that, in the aftermath of the ecumenical concerns of the Second Vatican Council, the new discipline was developed in a document of the Roman curia issued with the approval of Pope Paul VI (Congregation for the Doctrine of the Faith, instruction *Matrimonii sacramentum*, March 18, 1966 [*Acta Apostolicae Sedis* 58 (1966): 235-239]), and in a later papal document (Paul VI, motu proprio *Matrimonia mixta*, March 31, 1970 [*Acta Apostolicae Sedis* 62 (1970): 257-263]).

[25] *Sacri Canones*: ". . . attention should well be given to all of the things committed [in the new Eastern code] to the particular law of each of the Churches *sui iuris*, which are not considered necessary to the common good of all the Eastern Churches." There are many such instances in the code.

[26] Canon 815 parallels canon 1126 of the Latin code, except that the latter leaves this responsibility to the conferences of bishops for their respective regions.

joined upon the other spouse (namely, the one who is not within the full Catholic communion). She or he must be made aware of the promises only as a responsibility of the Catholic spouse (no. 2).

The content of the promise is twofold: that the Catholic spouse be "prepared to remove dangers of falling away from the faith" and "to do all in his or her power to have all the offspring baptized and educated in the Catholic Church." While the maintenance of faith by the Catholic spouse (the first part of the promises) is certainly important, the second clause concerning children is the more problematic.

A full commentary might explore each phrase of the promise to see to the Catholic baptism and upbringing of offspring, but the language can be taken in the conventional sense. This is not true, however, of the words "all in his or her power," translated from the Latin *omnia pro viribus*.

This language of the canon acknowledges that the promise cannot be an absolute or one that is susceptible of fulfillment in all cases and circumstances. To explore all the dimensions of the words, "all in his or her power" would far exceed the possibilities of this paper.[27] Even diverse translations might be considered: "in accord with his or her power," "depending on his or her power," "to the extent of his or her power."

As broadly drawn, the promise can have diverse meanings in the marriage of Catholics with other Christians of diverse Churches, ecclesial communities, denominations, or even sects.

Above all, the promise certainly has a distinct application in the case of the marriage of a Catholic with Eastern Christians who are not in full communion with the Catholic Church. This application is principally supported by the way in which the Second Vatican Council affirmed communion, albeit imperfect, of all Eastern Christians and Western Catholics. The whole matter is treated expansively in the conciliar decree on ecumenism.[28]

---

[27] For a succinct commentary, see Doyle, as cited in footnote 15 above, 802-804, with the references given there, especially Ladislas Örsy, "Religious Education of Children of Mixed Marriages," *Gregorianum* 45 (1964): 739-760.

[28] *Unitatis redintegratio* 14-18. In canonical discipline, this special character or status of the Eastern Churches (as contrasted with the Churches and ecclesial communities of the non-Catholic Western tradition) is also exemplified in the norm on sacramental sharing, specifically of the holy Eucharist, penance, and anointing of the sick. See canon 671, §3, parallel to the Latin code's canon 844, §3. The canon is derived from the conciliar decrees *Orientalium Ecclesiarum* 27 and *Unitatis redintegratio* 15. It should be stressed that this limited openness by the Catholic Church to such sacramental sharing with the faithful of the Eastern Churches should never be understood as commending or inviting Eastern Christians to transgress their own canonical discipline in this regard; see §5 of each of the parallel canons just mentioned.

Perhaps the following excerpt from a 1970 statement of the Orthodox/ Roman Catholic Consultation in the United States will provide the most useful observation on the subject:

> One area in which counseling by the pastors is desirable is the Christian upbringing of the children. We recognize the responsibility of each partner to raise their children in the faith of their respective Churches. We encourage the pastors of both Churches to counsel these couples in the hope of helping to resolve the problem which this responsibility creates. Specific decisions should be made by the couple only after informed and serious deliberation. Whether the decision is made to raise the children in the Orthodox or Catholic tradition, both partners should take an active role in the Christian upbringing of the children and in establishing their marriage as a stable Christian union. The basis for this pastoral counsel is not religious indifferentism, but our conviction of a common participation in the mystery of Christ and his Church.[29]

This position, which shows the underlying concern on the Catholic side over the meaning or extent of "all in his or her power,"[30] reflects only the judgment of the participants in the consultation. It was prepared as a part of the Catholic dialogue with the Orthodox, but it has significance and application for the dialogue with the Oriental Orthodox. The same is true of a document prepared a decade later, which includes the following paragraphs:

> The Orthodox/Roman Catholic couple contemplating marriage should discuss the spiritual formation of children with both pastors. Both parents should be urged to take an active role in their children's spiritual formation in all its aspects. Pastors should counsel the parents, and their children as well, against indifference in religious matters, which so often masks itself as tolerance. Since unity in

---

[29] "An Agreed Statement on Mixed Marriages," New York, May 20, 1970. In Joseph A. Burgess and Jeffrey Gros, eds., *Building Unity: Ecumenical Dialogues with Roman Catholic Participation in the United States (Ecumenical Documents IV)* (New York: Paulist, 1989), 326.

[30] As has been indicated earlier, this style of promise by the Catholic partner to a mixed marriage antedates both the 1983 Latin code and the 1990 Eastern code.

Christ through the Spirit is the ultimate basis and goal of family life, all members of the family should be willing, in a spirit of love, trust, and freedom, to learn more about their faith. They should agree to pray, study, discuss, and seek unity in Christ, and to express their commitment to this unity in all aspects of their lives.

Decisions, including the initial and very important one of the children's church membership, rest with both husband and wife and should take into account the good of the children, the strength of the religious convictions of the parents and other relatives, the demands of their consciences, the unity and stability of the family, and other aspects of the specific context. In some cases, when it appears certain that only one of the partners will fulfill his or her responsibility, it seems clear that the children should be raised in that partner's Church. In other cases, however, the children's spiritual formation may include a fuller participation in the life and traditions of both Churches, respecting, however, the canonical order of each Church. Here particularly the decision of the children's church membership is more difficult to make. Yet we believe that this decision can be made in good conscience. *This is possible because of the proximity of doctrine and practice of our Churches, which enables each to see the other precisely as* Church, as the locus for the communion of men and women with God and with each other through Jesus Christ in the Holy Spirit . . . .[31]

We are also aware that our joint recommendations on the formation of children of marriages between Orthodox and Roman Catholics differ in certain respects from the present legislation and practice of our Churches.[32] Yet we believe that our position is theologically and pastorally sound. Therefore we would urge our respective hierarchies to consider ways of reformulating legislation and pastoral

---

[31] Emphasis added. This is the reason for carefully distinguishing the case of the marriages of Catholics with Eastern Christians from marriages involving non-Catholic Western Christians, as mentioned already, especially in the light on the Catholic side of the conciliar decree *Unitatis redintegratio* 14-18.

[32] For Catholics, whether Eastern or Latin, the canonical situation has not been changed, so far as the written law is concerned, by the promulgation of the two codes.

guidelines in this area and of communicating this on the parish level, so that the spiritual growth of both the partners and the children of such marriages may be better fostered.[33]

The above statement places considerable stress upon the religious life and practice of the respective parents as a determinant. Specifically, if either parent is truly deficient in Christian practice, the responsibility devolves upon the other, whether it is the Orthodox or the Catholic spouse—and regardless of the promise made. Moreover, what is said of "the proximity of doctrine and practice" of the Catholic and Orthodox Churches is likewise applicable to the Oriental Orthodox and Catholic Churches. In the minds of the consultation members responsible for the previous statement, the problem is greatly lessened in the so-called mixed marriage of a Catholic and a Christian believer of the Eastern Christian traditions.

Neither the National Conference of Catholic Bishops in the United States nor the Apostolic Roman See has taken further legislative action since this statement was made. The resolution for the moment, again on the Catholic side, may be found in two distinct directions: first, the exercise by Catholic eparchial or diocesan bishops of their power to dispense from general or common laws, in this case dispensation from the canon requiring the promises;[34] and second, the legitimate (and virtuous) use of *epieikeia* or *epiky*, namely, in circumstances where the non-observance of an ecclesiastical law may be morally preferable to its observance.

c. 1993 Ecumenical Directory. A supplemental reference to what has been said about mixed marriages, and specifically about the question of the promises required of the Catholic spouse, is the recently revised directory on ecumenical matters issued by the Pontifical Council for Promoting Christian Unity and confirmed and approved by Pope John Paul II: *Directory for the Application of Principles and Norms on Ecumenism.*[35] This document, prepared for both Latin and Eastern Catholic Churches, is a revision and updating of the directory which originally appeared in two parts in 1967 and 1970.

Among many other matters, the new directory deals directly with the problems raised by the promises:

---

[33]   "Joint Recommendations on the Spiritual Formation of Children of Marriages between Orthodox and Roman Catholics," New York, October 11, 1980. In *Building Unity,* 340-341.

[34]   Canon 1538, §1 (parallel to canon 87, §1, of the Latin code), derived from the conciliar Decree on the Pastoral Office of Bishops in the Church *Christus Dominus,* October 28, 1965, no. 8b.

[35]   Vatican City, March 25, 1993. Both English and French versions were published.

The other party [the one who is not a Catholic] is to be informed of these promises and responsibilities. At the same time, it should be recognized that the non-Catholic party may feel a like obligation because of his/her own Christian commitment. It is to be noted that no formal written or oral promise is required of this partner in canon law.

Those who wish to enter a mixed marriage should, in the course of the contacts that are made in this connection, be invited and encouraged to discuss the Catholic baptism and education of the children they will have, and where possible come to a decision on this question before marriage.

In order to judge the existence or otherwise of a "just and reasonable cause" with regard to granting permission for this marriage, the local Ordinary will take account, among other things, of an explicit refusal on the part of the non-Catholic party (no. 150).

This exposition deserves a word of comment. Without retreating from the requirement that the Catholic party promise to do all in her or his power to see to the Catholic baptism and education of children, the directory does recognize that this promise may be incompatible with the Christian commitment of the non-Catholic within her or his own communion. The directory deals with the possible explicit rejection of the Catholic baptism and education of children in rather carefully crafted language: the local hierarch "will take account, among other things, of [this refusal]" when making the decision whether to permit the lawful celebration. This language is considerably different from the suggestion that, even in the extreme case of an explicit rejection of the Catholic party's responsibility, the bishop's permission must simply be refused.

Next the directory elaborates, in a tone similar to the passages already quoted from ecumenical consultations in the United States, on the actual situation which may prevail in mixed marriages:

In carrying out this duty of transmitting the Catholic faith to the children, the Catholic parent will do so with respect for the religious freedom and conscience of the other parent and with due regard for the unity and permanence of the marriage and for the maintenance of the communion of the family. If, notwithstanding the Catholic's best efforts ["all in his or her power"], the children are not baptized and brought up in the Catholic Church, the Catholic parent does not fall subject to the censure of canon law.[36] At the same time his/her obligation to share the Catholic faith with the children does not cease. It continues to make demands, which could be met, for example, by playing an active part in contributing to the Christian atmosphere of the home; doing all that is possible by word and example to enable the other members of the family to appreciate the specific values of the Catholic tradition; taking whatever steps are necessary to be well informed about his/her own faith so as to be able to explain and discuss it with them; praying with the family for the grace of Christian unity as the Lord wills it (no. 151).

The sections of the directory just quoted have an application, in varying decrees, to mixed marriages of Catholics with members of other Christian Churches and ecclesial communities in general, that is, whether of the East or West. The final paragraph of this section is directly applicable to the promises and responsibilities of the Catholic (Eastern or Latin) spouse in a marriage with an Eastern Christian not in full communion and speaks to our present concern:

> While keeping clearly in mind that doctrinal differences impede full sacramental communion between the Catholic Church and the various Eastern Churches, in the pastoral care of marriages between Catholics and Eastern Christians, particular attention should be given to the sound and consistent teaching of the faith which is shared by both and to the fact that in the Eastern Churches are to be found "true sacraments, and above all, by apostolic succession, the priesthood and the Eucharist, whereby they are still joined to us in closest intimacy."[37] If proper pasto-

---

[36]   A footnote in this section of the directory refers to canon 1366 of the Latin Church's code and canon 1439 of the Eastern code. In effect, the directory provides an authoritative statement that the Catholic parent in these circumstances should not fear being canonically penalized for having a child baptized and raised in another Christian communion.

[37]   A footnote in this section of the directory refers to *Unitatis redintegratio* 15, within the section of that conciliar decree expounding upon the distinctive relationship between the Catholic Church and the Churches of the East.

ral care is given to persons involved in these marriages, the faithful of both communions can be helped to understand how children born of such marriages will be initiated into and spiritually nourished by the sacramental mysteries of Christ. Their formation in authentic doctrine and ways of Christian living would, for the most part, be similar in each Church. Diversity in liturgical life and private devotion can be made to encourage rather than hinder family prayer (no. 152).

6. Other Questions[38]

a. Diriment or Invalidating Impediments. The several impediments to marriage, of both divine and ecclesiastical law, are enumerated with great specificity in canons 790-812 of the new Eastern code. In some instances, which need not be enumerated here, they differ from the parallel impediments in the Latin Church.

While unlikely, the possibility exists for additional matrimonial impediments in the canons of the autonomous Eastern Catholic Churches. But the development of these impediments is constrained by canon 792:

> The particular law of any Church *sui iuris* will not establish an impediment, unless for a most serious reason, after taking the counsel of other eparchial bishops of other Churches *sui iuris* to whom it is of interest and after consultation with the Apostolic See; no lower authority, however, can establish diriment impediments.

The norm illustrates the usefulness of a common code for all the autonomous Eastern Catholic Churches, while leaving a small opening for further particularization demanded by tradition or culture or custom of a given Church.

b. Pastoral Care. As suggested at the very beginning of this paper, the aspects of pastoral care, though not always satisfied, are hardly controversial. An article or section of the new code is devoted to this matter under the heading of "Pastoral care and those things which must precede the celebra-

---

[38] The matters in this section are not relegated to a small amount of space because they lack profound significance. Rather they deserve much greater treatment than is possible within the reasonable limits of this chapter.

tion of marriage" (canons 783-789). Unfortunately, nothing is said about the responsibility of the families and friends of those entering into Christian marriage and then living in Christian families—or indeed of the responsibility of the whole Christian community.[39]

Canon 783 defines the responsibility of "pastors of souls" both before marriage and during the married lives of their flock:

> §1. Pastors of souls are obliged to see to it that the Christian faithful are prepared for the matrimonial state:
>
> 1° by preaching and catechesis adapted to youths and adults, by which the Christian faithful are instructed concerning the meaning of Christian marriage and the obligations of spouses to each other and the primary right and obligation which parents have of doing all in their power to see to the physical, religious, moral, social, and cultural upbringing of their children;
>
> 2° by personal preparation of the parties for the marriage, by which they may be predisposed to that new state.
>
> §2. It is strongly recommended to the Catholic parties that they receive the Divine Eucharist in celebrating the marriage.[40]
>
> §3. After the marriage has been celebrated, pastors of souls should provide assistance to the couple, so that, while faithfully maintaining and protecting the conjugal covenant, they may day by day come to lead holier and fuller lives in their families.[41]

---

[39] The Latin Church's code is more expansive, especially in canon 1063 (corresponding to Eastern canon 783), which begins with the pastor's responsibility "to see to it that their own ecclesial community furnishes the Christian faithful assistance so that the matrimonial state is maintained in a Christian spirit and makes progress toward perfection." In fact, the Latin canons seem richer concerning catechesis, preparation, and celebration of marriage. This pastoral concern is supplemented in the liturgical law of the Roman rite, namely, in the ritual book for marriage, *Ordo celebrandi Matrimonium*, 2nd ed. (Vatican City, 1991), in its *praenotanda* or introduction, nos. 12 (the responsibility of the whole ecclesial community in the preparation for marriage) and 26 (again, the ministry of the whole Church and, in particular, of lay members).

[40] The late John Meyendorff, writing from a Byzantine perspective, noted: "Until the ninth century the Church did not know of any rite of marriage separate from the eucharistic liturgy. Normally, after entering a civil marriage, the Christian couple partook of the Eucharist, and this communion was—according to Tertullian—the seal of marriage." *Marriage: An Orthodox Perspective* (New York: St. Vladimir's Seminary Press, 1970), 27. In the Latin Church this liturgical tradition of completing marriage with the eucharistic celebration has been maintained from the ancient Western sacramentaries all the way to present-day rituals.

[41] §3 is taken directly from the Latin code, canon 1063, 4°.

The canon must be supplemented by a reference to the passages already quoted from the revised Roman ecumenical directory in its 1993 revision. The passages were presented in the context of the promises made prior to and responsibilities during a mixed marriage. They are equally appropriate under the heading of pastoral care.[42]

c. **Remarriage.** We would go too far afield to consider the new code's law on the dissolution of marriage, Pauline privilege, and indeed the nature of "annulment" of marriage as a declaration that a marriage was null and void from the beginning. We should, however, speak briefly of the differing Eastern and Western traditions regarding the celebration of marriage after divorce. This question is perhaps the principal barrier in the pastoral and even sacramental order (distinct from questions of ministries and primacy) to the restoration of full communion.

The Eastern code follows to the letter the received Latin Church law in this regard, however many the exceptions that might be found in Western church history. The norm is expressed in canon 853:

> The sacramental bond of marriage for a consummated marriage cannot be dissolved by any human power nor by any cause other than death.[43]

Some have felt that the repeated assertions, indeed asseverations, of the Second Vatican Council concerning the Eastern Churches in general and their traditional theologies and disciplines in particular might be interpreted as a recognition of the legitimacy, at least in the Eastern Catholic Churches, of remarriage after divorce in certain circumstances. The references of the conciliar Fathers have already been noted but bear specific repetition in the language of the decree *Unitatis redintegratio*:

> (16) From the earliest times, moreover, the Churches of
> the East followed their own disciplines, sanctioned by the
> holy fathers and by synods, including ecumenical synods.

---

[42] See at note 35, especially what is said in no. 152 of the directory. Pastoral considerations are equally strong in the texts quoted from bilateral dialogues in the United States; see at notes 29 and 33.

[43] Latin canon 1141 says the same, but in slightly different (technical) words: "A ratified [*ratum*, i.e., sacramental] and consummated marriage cannot be dissolved by any human power or for any reason other than death." The concept of indissolubility of marriage as dependent upon both sacramental celebration and consummation is from the Western canonical (and theological) tradition; in the Catholic Church, "dispensation" from such sacramental but non-consummated marriages (i.e., their dissolution) is reserved to the Bishop of Rome.

This diversity of observances and customs is no obstacle at all to the Church's unity, indeed it adds to the Church's beauty and contributes greatly to carrying out its mission, as already recalled. Therefore this Holy Synod, to remove all doubt, declares that the Churches of the East, keeping in mind the necessary unity of the entire Church, have the power to govern themselves in accord with their own disciplines: these are more suited to the character of their faithful and better adapted to foster the good of souls. The perfect observance of this traditional principle, one not always followed, is part of what is absolutely required, as a kind of prior condition, for the restoration of unity.

(17) It is suitable to declare also about diverse theological expressions of doctrine what has been said already about legitimate diversity. In the investigation of revealed truth, different methods and approaches to understand and profess divine realities have been used in the East and in the West. It is thus not surprising that sometimes certain aspects of the revealed mystery are perceived more fittingly or expressed more clearly by one tradition rather than the other. Thus these varied theological formulations are not rarely to be considered as complementary rather than opposed. . . .

This Holy Synod gives thanks to God that many Eastern sons and daughters of the Catholic Church, who preserve this patrimony and wish to live it more faithfully and completely, are already living in full communion with their brothers and sisters who follow the Western tradition.[44] But the Holy Synod declares that this entire patrimony, spiritual and liturgical, disciplinary and theological, belongs to the full catholicity and apostolicity of the Church in its diverse traditions.

---

[44] Entirely aside from the matter of matrimonial discipline, this sentence indicates movingly the careful balance that must be kept by the Catholic Church: on the one hand, recognizing the ecclesial reality of the Churches of the East with which our communion, though real, is less than complete, whether these are the Oriental Orthodox Churches or the Orthodox Church; on the other hand, asserting in equally solemn manner the ecclesial reality of the Eastern Catholic Churches to which the sentence refers. Progress toward full Christian unity has enabled the Churches not now in full communion to see one another in the metaphor of "sister Churches." A *fortiori* the several Catholic Churches *sui iuris*, whether Eastern or Latin, see one another as sister Churches.

(18) After taking all these matters into consideration, this sacred synod renews what past councils as well as bishops of Rome have declared: in order to restore or preserve communion and unity, one must "not impose any burden beyond what is necessary" (Acts 15: 28). . . .

These words may be interpreted to implicate respect for the Eastern tradition of marriage: That tradition is that the holy sacrament of marriage in Christ through the power of the Holy Spirit is indissoluble but in certain circumstances, where through human weakness the marriage has certainly failed and is no longer seen as the sign or mystery of the union of Christ and the Church, the divine mercy may be invoked and another marital union allowed. It is nonetheless unrealistic to expect that this position, seemingly well within the compass of the conciliar decree, would be accepted by the Catholic Church in the foreseeable future.

Thus, it seems wrong to encourage the Eastern Churches, including the Eastern Catholic Churches, to hope for the removal of this obstacle, pastorally significant as it is in the case of certain mixed marriages. We must also recall that the general councils of the West, considered ecumenical by the Catholic Church, have carefully avoided any direct or explicit rejection of the doctrine or practice of the East permitting a second marriage after divorce. This is true of Florence (1438-1445), of Trent (1545-1563), and of Vatican II (1962-1965).

Conclusion

Many other aspects of church order regarding Christian marriage might be taken up, with a view to seeking convergence rather than divergence between the Catholic Church (here understood as the Latin Church and the several Eastern Catholic Churches which are in full communion) and the several other Churches of the East, including those called the Oriental Orthodox Churches. While several instances of divergence are serious, they need not always affect the living out of the Christian faith in a mixed marriage. Included among these divergences are the differing understandings of Christian marriage, the Latin identification of sacrament and covenant/contract, and even the very different perceptions of the minister or ministers of the sacrament.

In the case of the pastoral care of prospective spouses and of Christian families, especially as carried out by the priests of the Church, there seems to be no room for basic disagreement. In cases where Latin and Eastern Catholic canon law offers no exceptions on the permanence of the sacramental marriage bond, there appears to be no ready or immediate resolution. On the other hand, the ready recognition by the Catholic Church, Latin and Eastern Catholic, of the validity and sacramental authenticity of celebrations of marriage in the other Eastern Churches is a positive sign—a sign, it is hoped, which will be reciprocated. And the admirable efforts to resolve the question of the Christian upbringing of children surely will bear fruit. ∼

The Official Oriental Orthodox–Roman Catholic Consultation in the United States of America

by Reverend Aelred Cody, OSB

At the end of their historic meeting in Rome in May 1970, Vasken I, the Supreme Patriarch and Catholicos of All Armenians, and Paul VI, the Roman Pontiff, issued a common declaration that urged theologians of their two Churches to come together for common study, promising their support of such efforts and their blessing upon them.[1] In Europe this exhortation was acted upon quickly. Already in September 1971 the first "Nonofficial Ecumenical Consultation between Theologians of the Oriental Orthodox and the Roman Catholic Churches," organized by the *Pro Oriente* foundation, convened in Vienna.[2] Four other meetings of this consultation were to follow in Vienna in 1973, 1976, 1978, and 1988.[3] The first two focused on christological questions, while subsequent meetings moved to a wider range of topics. The meetings included representatives not only of the Armenian Apostolic Church but of the other Oriental Orthodox Churches as well. These Viennese consultations were not official, which is to say that their participants were not officially appointed by the hierarchical authorities of their respective Churches.[4]

---

[1] The official text, in French, is published in *Acta Apostolicae Sedis* 62 (1970) 416-417. *The Vienna Dialogue* (see note 4 below), vol. 1, p. 107, gives an English version. His Holiness Vasken I died in Yerevan on August 18, 1994, sixteen years after Pope Paul VI's death on August 6, 1978.

[2] *Papers and Minutes of the First Vienna Consultation between Theologians of the Oriental Orthodox Churches and the Roman Catholic Church, September 7th-12th, 1971. Wort und Wahrheit,* Supplementary Issue 1 (Vienna: Herder Verlag, 1972).

[3] The volumes containing the papers and minutes of these meetings have the same title as the volume resulting from the first meeting (see the previous note), except for the order of the meetings and their dates—the second, September 3-9, 1973; the third, August 30-September 5, 1976; the fourth, September 11-17, 1978; the fifth, September 18-25, 1988. They are *Wort und Wahrheit,* Supplementary Issues 2-5 (Vienna: Herder Verlag, 1974, 1976, 1978, 1988). *Pro Oriente* has recently published a one-volume selection of papers from the five meetings.

[4] Useful summaries of the papers, discussion, and other proceedings of the five Viennese meetings, with the texts of their concluding communiqués and some valuable introductions and supplements, have been published as *The Vienna Dialogue: Five* Pro Oriente *Consultations with Oriental Orthodoxy* (2 vols.; Vienna: Pro Oriente, n.d.). These volumes have also been published in Arabic and in Malayalam.

1. The Origin of the Official Consultation in the United States

In the United States, the consultation between the Oriental Orthodox Churches and the Catholic Church was organized as an official consultation. Its members were to be officially appointed by their hierarchical authorities, who might themselves be members. The American consultation did not begin its work, however, until 1978, almost seven years after the first Viennese meeting and more than ten years after the organization of the official consultation of the Eastern, or Chalcedonian, Orthodox Churches and the Roman Catholic Church in this country.

It was, in fact, at a meeting of the Eastern Orthodox-Roman Catholic Consultation at Garrison, N.Y. in January 1976 that the idea of organizing an analogous consultation with the Oriental Orthodox Churches was discussed seriously by two of the Catholics present, Cardinal William Baum and Dr. Thomas E. Bird. Cardinal Baum was at that time the Archbishop of Washington and the Catholic prelate responsible for relations of the American Catholic hierarchy with the Eastern Churches, and Dr. Bird was professor of Slavic languages and literatures in Queens College of the City University of New York.[5] During that meeting, Cardinal Baum asked Dr. Bird to be the executive secretary of a dialogue, yet to be organized, between the Oriental Orthodox Churches and the Catholic Church.

Dr. Bird began by contacting the Armenian Apostolic Church, the largest of the Oriental Orthodox Churches in the Western Hemisphere and the first to be organized with a hierarchy of its own in America. He called formally on Archbishop Torkom Manoogian, the present Armenian Patriarch of Jerusalem, who was at that time Primate of the Eastern Diocese of the Armenian Church of America. Archbishop Torkom immediately expressed both his interest in the proposal and his willingness to make organizational moves on the Oriental Orthodox side. In May 1976, at a reception in honor of His Holiness [Patriarch] Ignatius Yacoub III, Syrian Orthodox Patriarch of Antioch and All the East, Dr. Bird spoke informally with Mor Athanasius Yeshue Samuel, Syrian Orthodox Archbishop of America and Canada, and to Fr. Marcos of the Coptic Orthodox Church. To both of them he communicated Cardinal Baum's hope, and both responded quite positively.

He also spoke with Archbishop Karekin Sarkissian, presently the Supreme Patriarch and Catholicos of All Armenians, who was at that time the Cilician

---

5   The historian of our consultation must base his work on minutes, official lists, and other unpublished documents, as well as on memories and personal notes. To enable me to document the beginning of the consultation and its first three years, Dr. Bird, thoroughly involved in the consultation from the outset, has given me access to his own notes and papers. For his helpful kindness I am very grateful.

jurisdiction's prelate in America. Archbishop Karekin was interested in the prospect of official conversations with Catholics, but his jurisdiction, the Armenian Apostolic Church of America (the Armenian Prelacy in America), has not been involved in the consultation. Political tensions within the communities of the Armenian diaspora continue to be reflected in the jurisdictional division of Armenian parishes and institutions in America, some subject to the Supreme Catholicos and Patriarch of All Armenians at Etchmiadzin in the Republic of Armenia, others subject to the Catholicos of the Great House of Cilicia, whose see is now at Antelias in Lebanon.[6] It became clear that an official consultation could not include both Armenian jurisdictions in this country, and that it could correctly be formed only with The Armenian Church of America, subject ultimately to the Supreme Catholicos in Etchmiadzin.

Because of the somewhat similar division of the Syrian Orthodox Church in South India,[7] a division extending to that Church's American communities, the official consultation would include those Indians of the Syrian Orthodox Church who are subject ultimately to the Syrian Orthodox Patriarch of Antioch and All the East but not those subject to the Catholicos of the Malankara Orthodox Syrian Church in India.

After those initial contacts made in the first half of 1976, Cardinal Baum invited Archbishop Torkom to a meeting in which the two of them, with other prelates and advisors whom they would invite from their respective Churches, would discuss the project of an official consultation. The meeting took place at a luncheon in the Gold Room of the Bellevue-Stratford Hotel in Philadelphia, August 4, 1976, during the Eucharistic Congress held in that city. Cardinal Baum and Archbishop Torkom presided over the meeting. Also present were of the Armenian Church, Archbishop Tiran Nersoyan, Bishop Papken Varjabedian, the Very Rev. Fr. Zaven Arzoumanian, and the Rev. Frs. Nersess Jebejian and Mampre Kouzouian; of the Catholic Church, Cardinal Johannes Willebrands, Bishop (now Cardinal) Bernard Law, Msgr. James G. Gillen, Frs. Gabriel Duffy, Edward Kilmartin, SJ, and J. Peter Sheehan, and the executive secretary, Dr. Thomas E. Bird.

---

[6] Historical documents important for the history of this American schism from 1914, when problems were beginning, until 1949 have been published in English (in most cases as translations from an Armenian original), with brief introductions explaining their historical contexts, as *Documents on the Schism in the Armenian Church of America* (New York: Diocese of the Armenian Church of America, 1993). The Prelacy became a jurisdiction of the Catholicate of the Great House of Cilicia in 1957. Efforts to heal the schism continue.

[7] See J. Madey, "Background and History of the Present Schism in the Malankara Church," *Oriens christianus* 60 (1976) 95-112.

In this meeting in Philadelphia, it was agreed that the projected American consultation should try to respond to the exhortation of Catholicos Vasken I and Pope Paul VI that the theologians of their two Churches devote themselves to concurrent study. No specific plan for their doing so was created then, however. Each of the two presiding officers named an executive committee for his Church: Bishop Papken and Fr. Mesrob Semerjian for the Armenian Church; and Dr. Bird and Fr. Sheehan for the Catholic Church. The two committees were to maintain contact and decide what shape the proposed dialogue should take. At this early stage the dialogue was foreseen as one in which only two Churches, the Armenian Apostolic Church and the Roman Catholic Church, would be directly involved. Archbishop Torkom would keep the authorities of the other Oriental Orthodox Churches in the United States informed of what was happening, and representatives of those other Churches would be invited to attend meetings as observers, in a system of rotation. When the consultation actually began its work, however, it included all of the Oriental Orthodox Churches in the United States—except, for the reasons noted above, the American dioceses of the Armenian Catholicate of Cilicia and of the Malankara Orthodox Syrian Church.

2. The Planning Meetings

The executive committees appointed in Philadelphia in 1976 organized two planning meetings. The first of them was held June 17, 1977 in the offices of the National Conference of Catholic Bishops in Washington, with Armenian Bishop Zaven Chinchinian and Catholic Bishop J. Francis Stafford presiding. (At that time, Francis Stafford was an auxiliary bishop in Baltimore, but he is now the Archbishop of Denver.) Also there for the meeting were Bishop Papken Varjabedian and Fr. Zaven Arzoumanian of the Armenian Church, and Dr. Thomas Bird and Fr. J. Peter Sheehan of the Catholic Church. The participants decided that papers to be given in the meetings for which they were planning should deal with historical, theological, and pastoral questions.

A second, much larger planning meeting was held January 27, 1978 in the offices of the Armenian Diocese in New York, with Archbishop Torkom and Bishop Stafford presiding, and with those present at the first planning meeting present again. New from the Armenian Church were Frs. Arten Ashjian, Michael Buttero, and Karekin Kasparian. For the first time the Syrian Orthodox Church was represented, by Archbishop Athanasius Yeshue Samuel and Fr. K. M. Simon. Fr. Robert Taft, SJ, was new on the Catholic side. Cardinal Baum, Archbishop Tiran, and Frs. Duffy, Kilmartin, and

Sheehan, all of whom who had been at the introductory meeting in Philadelphia, were also present at this meeting. Participants discussed the topics the consultation should or should not address, and they enunciated the working principle that on any topic two papers should be read, one by an Oriental Orthodox and one by a Catholic.

It was in this second and final planning meeting that the important decision was made, with complete agreement on both sides, that on the Orthodox side of the consultation all of the Oriental Orthodox Churches would be included. The consultation would not be an Armenian Orthodox-Roman Catholic consultation but "The Oriental Orthodox-Roman Catholic Consultation in the United States of America." The inclusion of the final phrase "in the United States of America" was intentional. Archbishop Torkom had noted that it should be clear that the consultation represented our Churches officially in the United States but not necessarily in other countries. His reasoning was that both Oriental Orthodox and Catholic Churches have authorities in other parts of the world who could be disturbed by actions taken or statements made by the consultation.

With Archbishop Torkom's appointment of Fr. Arten Ashjian as executive secretary of the Oriental Orthodox side of the consultation, and Bishop Stafford's appointment of Dr. Thomas Bird as executive secretary of the Catholic side, the planning stage was finished, and the Official Oriental Orthodox-Roman Catholic Consultation in the United States of America was established. Four months later the first of its series of working meetings was held.

3. The Members

Since then, there has been both continuity and change in the membership of the consultation. Archbishop Torkom assumed the official status of an observer rather than a member; as such, he retained an active interest in the consultation and its progress until he was elected Patriarch of Jerusalem in 1990. The first chairman of the Oriental Orthodox group was Bishop Papken Varjabedian. In 1989 the Oriental Orthodox members of the consultation elected Chorepiscopus John Meno of the Syrian Church as their chairman, with Fr. Garabed Kochakian of the Armenian Church as vice-chairman. Bishop J. Francis Stafford was the chairman of the Catholic group until he was succeeded by Bishop Howard J. Hubbard of Albany in 1985. The chairmen of the two groups are the co-chairmen of the consultation's meetings.

The Catholic group's coordinator has always been an associate director of the Catholic Bishops' Committee for Ecumenical and Interreligious Affairs. The coordinator was first Fr. Peter Sheehan, succeeded by Fr. Joseph W. Witmer. Then, from the end of 1987 until his death in 1990, Fr. Thaddeus D. Horgan, SA, was coordinator, followed by Brother Jeffrey Gros, FSC, who already knew many of the consultation's Oriental Orthodox participants.[8] Fr. Arten Ashjian has coordinated the Oriental Orthodox group from the beginning. In 1994, Archbishop Khajag named Fr. Haigazoun Najarian the Armenian Diocese's ecumenical officer and the consultation's Oriental Orthodox coordinator during Fr. Arten's leave of absence for work on a special project.

Some of the persons who were involved in the planning meetings stayed on as members of the consultation, once it began its working sessions. Some of them—Dr. Thomas Bird and Fr. Gabriel Duffy among the Catholics, and Fr. Arten Ashjian among the Oriental Orthodox—remain members of the consultation to this day. Among the first members of the consultation, death has claimed Archbishop Tiran Nersoyan of the Armenian Church in 1989, Fr. Gabriel Abdelsayed, the Coptic patriarchal vicar, in 1993, Fr. Edward Kilmartin, SJ, in 1994, and Archbishop Athanasius Yeshue Samuel in 1995. Others, including Bishop Papken Varjabedian, Frs. Zaven Arzoumanian, Michael Buttero, Robert Taft, SJ, and Karekin Kasparian, are no longer members of the consultation.

Since the completion of the planning stage, new members have been appointed to the consultation at various times. Some of them are no longer members: Frs. Avak Assadourian and Arnak Kasparian, Dr. Krikor Maksoudian and Dr. Hagop Nersoyan of the Armenian Church; Frs. Aidan Kavanagh, OSB, and Joseph Thomas of the Catholic Church; and Archbishop Yesehaq, Fr. Haddis Gedey, Mr. Wolde Hawarian Smythe, and Fr. Tsehai Birhanu of the Ethiopian Church. Others are members of the consultation today: of the Armenian Church, Fr. Khajag Barsamian (now Archbishop Khajag, elected primate of the Eastern Diocese in 1990), Frs. Mardiros Chevian, Garabed Kochakian, Haigazoun Najarian, and Deacon Aren Jebejian; of the Catholic Church, Frs. Aelred Cody, OSB, Sarhad Hermiz Jammo, John Long, SJ, and Ronald Roberson, CSP; of the Coptic Church, Frs. Tadros Malaty, David Bibawi, Yacob Ghaly, and Athanasius K. Farag; of the Ethiopian Church, Archbishop Matthias; and of the Syrian Church, Chorepiscopus John Meno.

---

[8]   In 1985, when the Commission on Faith and Order of the National Council of the Churches of Christ in the U.S.A. organized a meeting of Eastern and Oriental Orthodox, Catholic, Anglican, and Protestant scholars to discuss topics of christology, Brother Jeffrey Gros was director of the commission. He wrote the introduction to the meeting's published papers, *Christ in East and West,* edited by Paul R. Fries and Tiran Nersoyan (Macon, Ga.: Mercer University Press, 1987).

4. Falterings and Renewed Commitment
One cannot claim that the dialogue has always continued with unabated enthusiasm. Many of the consultation's members have at various times wondered whether it should continue. Different members have expected different things of the dialogue, and these different expectations have not always been clearly perceived and understood within the large group. To some, the results have seemed disappointingly meager. Between the January and December meetings of 1984, Archbishop Torkom and Bishop Stafford met and took some well-pondered administrative steps which tackled some of these problems. Their work was clear evidence of their conviction of the dialogue's importance for their Churches. By and large, disillusionment of this sort requires not administrative action but personal adjustment and open discussion. In the consultation, such discussion has typically taken place in separate caucuses of the Oriental Orthodox members and the Catholic members, who then came together to communicate the thoughts expressed in the caucuses and to continue the discussion.

The planned celebration of the consultation's tenth anniversary in New York in 1988 did not include a regular working meeting in connection with the festivities, but did include Fr. Aelred Cody's review of the first decade and the preceding years of planning. The celebration never took place. In April 1989 the Oriental Orthodox members met to discuss the dialogue seriously and to ask themselves whether they thought that its continuation was worthwhile and whether they could, and should, continue to support it. Their conclusion turned out to be unanimously in favor of doing so. The following June, the Oriental Orthodox and the Catholic members met together at the Armenian Diocesan Center in New York to review the past and to think about the future. Fr. Garabed Kochakian's list of worthwhile topics for future meetings, topics having to do particularly with marriage and with theological issues related to it, found favor with everyone present.

The meeting in Washington in February 1990 was very poorly attended, mainly because extremely bad weather made travel impossible for many. Archbishop Torkom was called to Jerusalem, where he was soon to be elected patriarch. Fr. Khajag Barsamian from New York, who had been appointed an Oriental Orthodox member of the consultation and had become an active and engaged participant, succeeded Archbishop Torkom as primate, a position which left him little time for other activities. Not long after the meeting in February Fr. Thaddeus Horgan, the Catholic coordinator, died. After suffering these losses, the consultation languished.

It began to move forward again when Brother Jeffrey Gros, FSC, became Fr. Thaddeus's successor in the National Conference of Catholic Bishops' Secretariat for Ecumenical and Interreligious Affairs. With the co-chairmen's authorization, Brother Jeffrey and Fr. Arten Ashjian, active once again in the consultation despite his retirement, organized a small planning committee made up of the following members: Archbishops Khajag and Yesehaq; Frs. Aelred Cody, Teklemariam Greene of the Ethiopian Church, and Garabed Kochakian; the co-chairmen, Bishop Hubbard and Chorepiscopus John Meno; and the coordinators, Fr. Arten and Brother Jeffrey. This committee met in the offices of the Armenian Diocese April 10, 1992. Fr. Aelred Cody drew up a list of suggested topics for the future with a long-range goal (the unity of our Churches) and various short-range goals. Participants discussed these topics for the first time (before the topics were discussed again in the meeting of the entire consultation that followed), further topics were suggested, some practical projects were planned, and the next plenary meeting's agenda and date, September 15-16, 1992, were set.

When the entire consultation came together in September, it became clear that the individual members, and the two sides of the consultation as groups, had a sense of mutual ease and trust, as well as a confidence in hierarchical support. Members of the consultation felt and said that a preliminary phase of dialogue in the United States was finished, that the Churches had managed to go beyond their basic theological knowledge of one another to an appreciative ecclesial knowledge of one another, and that they had established a good atmosphere for dealing with problems together. The dialogue had clearly been resumed with fresh vitality.

5. Papers Prepared and Problems Discussed

In the first working meeting, May 26-27, 1978, Fr. Edward Kilmartin presented a paper on ways and means, on the spirit in which the members of the consultation might well do their work. Fr. K. M. Simon presented a prepared response. Twice afterwards Fr. Kilmartin revised his paper, taking into account Fr. Simon's response and the discussions which took place in the meetings. As previously mentioned, participants in the first planning meeting decided that authors of papers prepared for and discussed in the meetings should deal with historical, theological, or pastoral topics. In the first working meeting it was further agreed that the study of liturgical topics should be part of the theological task since it would sharpen awareness of what is common to all of our Churches and what is different among them in ritual and sacramental practice and in theological understanding. The topics of most of the papers actually presented do fall within these categories.[9]

The papers on ecclesiastical history are clustered in the meeting of May 1978, when a member of each Oriental Orthodox Church presented a compact historical account of his own Church. In more recent meetings, attention has turned to contemporary historical developments that have an important bearing, direct or indirect, on relations between the Oriental Orthodox Churches and the Catholic Church. In September 1992 Fr. Ronald Roberson reported on the Vatican's principles and norms for coordinating Catholic evangelization and ecumenical relations in the nations of the former Soviet Union (including the Republic of Armenia). In June 1993 and May 1994, he generally analyzed contemporary relations between the Catholic Church and the Oriental Orthodox Churches.

Fr. John Long, in the September 1992 meeting, commented on two specific documents: the letter of March 29, 1977 sent by Cardinal Johannes Willebrands and Cardinal Paul Philippe to the Coptic Catholic Patriarch; and the *Principles for Guiding the Search for Unity between the Catholic Church and the Coptic Orthodox Church* signed by Pope John Paul II and Pope Shenouda III on June 23, 1979.[10] These official and highly authoritative documents have great implications for relations between all Oriental Orthodox Churches and the Roman Catholic Church. In them, faith is affirmed, ecumenical method is indicated, and proselytism is ruled out. In addition, the two popes envisage full recognition of one another's Churches and sacramental life, in a union without absorption or domination, with respect for each Church's right to govern itself according to its own laws and traditions.

The practice of having a member of each Church report new developments in his own Church has continued since its beginning in 1990. Most reports of developments promise life and hope, but both in 1992 and in 1993 Archbishop Yesehaq told of the distressing situation that has arisen in the Church of Ethiopia with its two claimants to the patriarchal throne. Members of the consultation were among the first people outside the Syrian Orthodox Church to share Archbishop Athanasius Yeshue Samuel's happiness

---

9   A complete list of the papers is given in the appendix at the end of this history.
10   These two documents have been privately printed in *The Roman Catholic Church and the Coptic Orthodox Church: Documents (1973-1978)* (Rome: Information Service of the Pontifical Council for Promoting Christian Unity, n.d.) 23-26, 30-32. The *Principles*, consisting of a preamble and a protocol, can be read in *The Vienna Dialogue*, vol. 1, pp. 111-114.

when the handsome Syrian Orthodox Book of Anaphoras and common order of the Divine Liturgy appeared in both Syriac and English.[11]

Papers on specifically liturgical topics have been presented in various meetings by Archbishop Yesehaq (1982), Chorepiscopus John Meno (May 1979), and Frs. Gabriel Abdelsayed (April 1980), Sarhad Jammo (January 1984), Aidan Kavanagh (November 1980), and Robert Taft (December 1979).[12] Archbishop Tiran Nersoyan has given lectures on the Armenian Church's divine liturgy and hours of common prayer. (These lectures were not prepared in the form of papers to be distributed to the members.) In most of the lectures, both history and theology had their part. Authors of papers on topics of sacramental theology and its historical development have been Frs. Gabriel Abdelsayed (September 1982), Aelred Cody (September 1982), Aidan Kavanagh (December 1985), Edward Kilmartin (December 1981), Garabed Kochakian (December 1985), and K. M. Simon (December 1981). Aspects of christology and their significance, past and present, in the lives of our Churches have been addressed by Archbishop Tiran (May 1979), Frs. Gabriel Duffy (May 1979) and Robert Taft (December 1978), and Dr. Hagop Nersoyan (December 1978). As the participants in the dialogue became more familiar with one another and more sensitive to sometimes unspoken concerns, they realized that many of these concerns had to do with pastoral issues and problems, or with what Archbishop Tiran in the second planning meeting had called "existential issues." In the years after the consultation got its bearings, such issues have been addressed in several of the papers prepared. The discussions following the presentations of these papers have probably been of greatest interest to members. In the meeting of December 1984, Fr. Arten Ashjian addressed the concern caused by the establishment of an exarchate for Armenian Catholics in the United States. This led to a serious and open discussion and, as we shall see, to the drafting of one of the consultation's statements.

More recently, in the meeting of June 1993, the members of the consultation discussed what seemed to be intentions of the Armenian Catholic Church to proselytize in newly independent Armenia. This potential proselytism had already elicited an encyclical of united concern signed by

---

[11] *Anaphoras: The Book of the Divine Liturgies According to the Rite of the Syrian Orthodox Church of Antioch,* translated from the original Syriac by Archdeacon Murad Saliba Barsom, edited and published by Metropolitan Mar Athanasius Yeshue Samuel, Archbishop of the Syrian Orthodox Church in the United States of America and Canada, 1991.

[12] The title of each paper can be found in the appendix under the date of the meeting in which it was presented and discussed.

Vasken I, Supreme Patriarch and Catholicos of All Armenians, and Karekin II, Catholicos of the Great House of Cilicia; had occasioned a telegram from Catholicos Vasken to the cardinal prefect of the Oriental Congregation in Rome; and had brought about a memorandum presented to the Roman authorities by a delegation of Armenian Orthodox prelates, including Archbishop Khajag.[13] In this lengthy discussion, the place of Eastern Catholics in relation both to Rome and to their Orthodox mother Churches, as well as the respective roles of all three Churches in such triangles, were examined frankly by the consultation's members, ultimately with better understanding all around.

Right after this meeting, Bishop Howard Hubbard, Catholic chairman of the consultation, wrote to Cardinal Edward Idris Caseate, President of the Pontifical Council for Promoting Christian Unity in Rome, to propose a message to the supreme patriarch and catholicos. The message would clearly state two points: that the principles and norms for the Catholic Church's evangelizing activity and ecumenical commitment in the countries of the former Soviet Union, issued the year before by the Pontifical Commission for Russia, apply to Armenia; and that the Vatican insists that there be no Catholic proselytizing among the Orthodox faithful of Armenia. Cardinal Caseate acted on Bishop Hubbard's proposal by sending a private letter, in the sense proposed, to Catholicos Vasken on July 5, 1993. Not long afterward, Bishop Hubbard personally visited the Pontifical Council for Promoting Christian Unity to press the ecumenical concerns of his letter in a matter whose potential seriousness, Cardinal Caseate and Bishop Duprey (the council's president and secretary) told him, had not been fully realized earlier.

A major pastoral concern of the consultation has been marriage of members of the Oriental Orthodox Churches with those of the Latin and Eastern Catholic Churches. For the meeting in June 1983, Fr. Kilmartin prepared a paper on Roman legislation for the celebration of marriage between a Catholic and a non-Catholic Eastern Christian, and Fr. Arten Ashjian prepared one on the Armenian Orthodox Church's approach to intermarriage and the problems and concerns raised by intermarriage in the Armenian diaspora. In the same meeting and in the following one, Fr. Gabriel Duffy explained the actual practice of American Catholic parishes and chanceries in dealing with cases of intermarriage. For the meeting in January 1984, Fr. Arten and Chorepiscopus John Meno prepared a paper on the Oriental Or-

---

[13] See the documents, of both the Armenian Catholic Church and the Armenian Orthodox Church, in English translation and in Armenian, in *The Mother Church and Roman Catholic Missionary Activity in a Reborn Armenia* (New York: St. Vartan Press, 1993).

thodox pastoral practice in such cases, and the same topic was addressed in the meeting of December 1984, in addition to Coptic and Ethiopian Orthodox practice.

The consultation returned to the topic of mixed marriages when Fr. Garabed Kochakian and Chorepiscopus John Meno, after discussion among Oriental Orthodox bishops and priests, presented a first draft of their *Guidelines for Oriental Orthodox/Roman Catholic Marriages* in September 1992. Second and third forms of their text, revised and augmented, were presented in June 1993 and May 1994. Each time, there was extended discussion of such matters as diverging theologies of the minister of the sacrament, grounds for annulment, different laws governing remarriage or successive marriage (if a particular Church allows it) and different rituals used for these marriages, and the sacramental character of the nuptial blessing. Close attention was given to differences of law and practice among the Oriental Orthodox Churches themselves. The final text of these important and helpful *Guidelines* can be found in this book.

6. Common Statements and a Resolution

From the September 1982 papers on eucharistic words of institution, anamnesis, and epiclesis by Frs. Gabriel Abdelsayed and Aelred Cody came *An Agreed Statement on the Eucharist*, which was first worked on in that meeting and refined in the meeting of June 1983. In its final form, it was sent to the authorities of our various Churches and given to the press.[14] The historical significance of this common statement may too easily be overlooked. Before our Churches were separated in the aftermath of the Council of Chalcedon, our shared view of the Eucharist and of eucharistic ritual was already in place. Afterwards, our theologians reflected on that shared view in isolation from one another and in defensive estrangement from one another. Never before in our divided history since 451 has such carefully pondered theological agreement on the Eucharist been reached and expressed in common accord.

Other statements were drawn up not to transcend the needless theological disagreement of past centuries but to respond to current situations. An *Agreed Statement on the Crisis of the Churches in Egypt and Lebanon*, pro-

---

[14]   The text was printed in many religious newspapers. It was also published in *Origins* 13 (1983-1984) 167-168, under a general heading in which the consultation is called the "Orthodox [not specifically "Oriental Orthodox"]-Roman Catholic Dialogue," although the participating Churches are correctly identified in an editorial introduction.

duced in the consultation's meeting in September 1982 and released to the press after the meeting in June 1983,[15] was sent to the following groups: the Vatican's Secretariat (now Pontifical Council) for Promoting Christian Unity; the presidents and general secretaries of the National Conference of Catholic Bishops and of the United States Catholic Conference; and the secretary and the African desk of the latter conference's Office of Social Development and World Peace. This statement was followed by a resolution, passed in the meeting of June 1983, on the grave situation of the Coptic Orthodox Church in Egypt, where Pope Shenouda III continued to be held under house arrest and Islamic militants continued to victimize Christians. The resolution—published by the U.S. Armenian and Syrian Churches and brought to the attention of the U.S. Catholic bishops in their meeting the following November—went before the Administrative Board of the United States Catholic Conference, which sent it to the Vatican, where it was diplomatically communicated to the appropriate officials.

In the December 1984 meeting, members discussed Fr. Arten Ashjian's paper concerning the establishment of an Armenian Catholic exarchate in the United States. In response, members attending the meeting drew up a statement of "concern, perplexity, and pain caused by the appointment of an Armenian Catholic exarch in the United States," and discussed a correct course of action. The text of the statement was immediately sent to Archbishop Torkom. When he had approved and signed it, he sent it to the authorities of the other Oriental Orthodox Churches in this country for their signatures before it was entrusted to Bishop Stafford as the Catholic chairman of the consultation. Bishop Stafford sent it with a cover letter to the Secretariat for Promoting Christian Unity in Rome. He sent a copy to the apostolic pro-nuncio in Washington and informed Bishop Nerses Setian, the newly appointed Armenian Catholic Exarch, of the steps being taken.

From the Secretariat for Promoting Christian Unity, Fr. (now Bishop) Pierre Duprey responded to Archbishop Torkom with words of assurance that the Holy See's sole reason for appointing an Armenian Catholic exarch was that of serving the Armenian Catholics in North America, and that no interest in proselytizing lay behind the appointment. Some readers of his response might have objected to the fact that he never suggested that the appointment of Eastern Catholic exarchs in America might cease. Members of the consultation were probably realistic enough not to expect immediate change as a result of their action. The Secretariat for Promoting Christian Unity was not

---

[15]   The text was published in *Origins* 13 (1983-1984) 168.

in a position to effect a change of policy or practice in such matters. For the Catholic members of the consultation, the most important result of this action might well have been their opportunity to better understand the distress which the existence of the Eastern Catholic Churches brings to Orthodox Christians. For the Oriental Orthodox members, the most important result might have been the experience of expressing their distress freely and receiving unfeigned support from the Catholic members. For both groups, this was an important occasion of solidarity in doing realistic and positive things to deal with that distress.

7. Practical Achievements

Among the consultation's practical achievements is the pamphlet on the Oriental Orthodox Churches edited by Fr. Taft, including material on each Church furnished by the Orthodox members of the consultation.[16] To help Catholic priests working with cases of mixed marriage, the pamphlet provides the names, addresses, and telephone numbers of the authorities of each Oriental Orthodox Church in the country who should be contacted. The Armenian Prelacy and the North American Metropolitanate of the Malankara Orthodox Syrian Church of India are included as well, since mixed marriages take place between Catholics and members of those two Oriental Orthodox jurisdictions, too. The book containing the present essay can also be counted among the practical results of the consultation's work. Finally, practical help was given to two Ethiopian Orthodox students by arranging scholarships enabling them to study in the Immaculate Conception Seminary in Huntington, N.Y.

Meetings of the consultation have also made it possible to clarify specific questions of jurisdiction or hierarchy within Oriental Orthodox Churches in order to help Roman Catholic authorities uncertain how to proceed correctly in a given situation. Some cases of vexation caused by illegitimate action on the part of a Catholic cleric have been brought to the consultation's attention. In the meeting of May 1987, Catholic Chairman Bishop Hubbard, unanimously and strongly supported by the other Catholic members of the consultation, invited the Oriental Orthodox to report any grievance arising from action or negligence on the part of a Catholic, with assurance that the Catholics of the dialogue would take steps to correct the cause of the grievance.

---

[16] *The Oriental Orthodox Churches in the United States,* edited by Robert F. Taft, SJ (Washington, D.C.: Secretariat for Ecumenical and Interreligious Affairs, National Conference of Catholic Bishops, 1986; distributed by the United States Catholic Conference).

8. Problems to Solve, Opportunities to Seize

As we think of the future, we may also ask ourselves about problems only partly resolved but now seen more clearly and better understood. Our American consultation has not dealt much with the christological issues which were the excuse for our division to begin with, because the common declarations of the Roman Catholic Popes Paul VI and John Paul II, the Armenian Catholicos Vasken I, the Syrian Patriarchs Ignatius Yacoub III and Ignatius Zakka I, and the Coptic Pope Shenouda III have together declared to all of us, with the high authority of their offices, that our christological faith is, after all, essentially the same, and that the christological differences lie mainly on the level of terminology.[17] Similar declarations related to the work of the Vienna dialogue are found in the joint communiqué of the Bishop of Rome and the Catholicos of the Great House of Cilicia,[18] and in the doctrinal agreement between the Malankara Syrian Orthodox Church and the Roman Catholic Church.[19]

We seem to remain divided largely because we have different systems of ecclesiastical organization, structure, and authority which we understandably defend by elevating them to the level of theological disagreement. In our official American dialogue we have not yet taken up questions of ecclesiology. We have not yet tried together to see how we might achieve consensus on the structure of the Church universal and the position of particular Churches within it, united but with fully accepted diversity of canonical systems and of sacramental practice. We have not yet examined ecclesiological issues like primacy and patriarchy, or the role which the Bishop of Rome might play in our Churches' relations when they are again in full communion with one another. If these are the issues that stand in the way of our reunion, then they must be addressed sooner or later.

One reason for our not addressing them is that, while our consultation is official, it engages only Churches in the United States. Among the Churches actually involved in our American consultation, the only official dialogue established at the universal level is the one in which the Coptic Orthodox

---

[17] The texts of these common declarations, in English, can be read in *The Vienna Dialogue*, vol. 1, p. 107 (Pope Paul VI and Catholicos Vasken I, May 12, 1970), p. 108 (Pope Paul VI and Patriarch Ignatius Yacoub III, October 27, 1971), pp. 109-110 (Pope Paul VI and Pope Shenouda III, May 10, 1973), pp. 117-119 (Pope John Paul II and Patriarch Ignatius Zakka I Iwas, June 23, 1984).

[18] *The Vienna Dialogue*, vol. 1, p. 115-116 (Pope John Paul II and Catholicos Karekin II, April 19, 1983).

[19] *The Vienna Dialogue*, vol. 1, pp. 123-124. This common text was adopted by the joint international commission for dialogue between the two Churches when it met in Kottayam, Kerala, October 22-25, 1989. A French version, with a brief editorial comment on some of its details and on its openness of attitude, can be found in *Irénikon* 63 (1990) 359-362.

Church and the Roman Catholic Church are partners.[20] It has recently been asked in our consultation, "To what extent are what the Official Oriental Orthodox-Roman Catholic Consultation in the United States of America says and what it achieves (its *Agreed Statement on the Eucharist*, for example) still limited to the United States of America?" Reasons of modesty may explain this limitation, but a certain amount of passivity may be involved also.[21] Conversely, a decision made at the highest level affecting two of our Churches—the authorization given by Roman Catholic Pope John Paul II and Mar Ignatius Zakka I of the Syrian Orthodox Church to the faithful of each of their Churches for receiving the sacraments of penance, Eucharist, and anointing of the sick from priests of the other Church when they need those sacraments but find it either materially or morally impossible to reach a priest of their own Church—has not been communicated effectively to bishops and parish priests of the Catholic Church in this country.[22] We need to engage our Churches more broadly, although all agree that we also need to be prudent in our manner of doing so.

In the immediate future, however, the members of the American consultation will probably maintain their present consensus that they will deal mainly with questions of the coexistence of our Churches in American society, mixed marriages and pastoral care, changes from one Church to another (whether as a result of proselytism or not), development of mutual understanding, and ways of being constructively helpful to one another.

---

[20] On the other side of the Atlantic, the *Pro Oriente* foundation has definitively concluded its series of unofficial consultations on christology, but it plans to continue promoting meetings between the Oriental Orthodox Churches and the Roman Catholic Church. These meetings are to be of two kinds: (1) symposia, in which knowledge of what has been achieved in the ecumenical dialogues will be communicated as widely as possible among the clergy and theologically engaged of particular regions, and (2) study seminars, in which the participants will examine more deeply the documents already produced and questions not fully answered; a standing committee of six Oriental Orthodox members and three Catholic members has been established to evaluate what has been done and to plan new actions (*Proche-Orient chrétien* 41 [1991] 346-347).

 Three study seminars have been held in or near Vienna, one, June 29-July 1, 1991, on primacy (see *Proche-Orient chrétien* 41 [1991] 433-434; *Irénikon* 64 [1991] 391), another, June 26-29, 1992, on councils and conciliarity (see *Irénikon* 65 [1992] 223-225), and a third, July 1-5, 1994, on ecclesiology and the unity of the Church. At Pope Shenouda III's invitation, a symposium for Egypt was held at the monastery of Amba Bishoi, October 26-28, 1991; the 120 participating bishops, priests, and theologians of the various ancient Churches did not limit themselves to discussion of the dialogue in Vienna (see *Irénikon* 64 [1991] 519-22). For India, a symposium was held at Kottayam, September 30-October 4, 1993, with 170 participants from ten different Churches.

[21] The fact that work on text of the agreed statement on the Eucharist had begun was noted in the international journal *Irénikon* 55 (1982) 552, but the final text of the statement has not been well circulated.

[22] This authorization is given in the common declaration which Pope John Paul II and Patriarch Ignatius Zakka I signed on June 23, 1984 (see note 17 above).

In any case, the Official Oriental Orthodox-Roman Catholic Consultation in the United States of America has grown into mellow maturity. With the patient and committed perseverance of our Churches and of the members of the consultation, we move onward, asking that God, effecting in us what is pleasing in his sight, equip us with everything good, that we may do his will (Heb 13:21). ⌒

APPENDIX

Papers Written for the Official Oriental Orthodox–Roman Catholic Consultation, 1978-1994[23]

May 1978
Gabriel A. Abdelsayed, "A Brief Account of the Coptic Orthodox Church."
Zaven Arzoumanian, "The Origins of Armenian Christianity."
Edward J. Kilmartin, SJ, "Purpose and Method of the Dialogue Between the Oriental Orthodox and Roman Catholic Churches."
L. M. Mandefro (now Archbishop Yesehaq), "The Ethiopian Church."
John Meno, "A Brief History of the Syrian Orthodox Church of Antioch and Her Faith."
K. M. Simon, "Response [to E. J. Kilmartin's Paper] on Behalf of the Oriental Orthodox Churches."

December 1978
Hagop Nersoyan, "How to Dissolve the Chalcedonian Controversy."
Robert F. Taft, SJ, "Did the Council of Chalcedon Add to or Alter the Church's Understanding of Christology?"

May 1979
Gabriel Duffy, "The Life and Teachings of Christ as They Are Interpreted, Understood, and Lived by a Roman Catholic."
Edward J. Kilmartin, SJ, "Purpose, Scope, and Method of the Dialogue Between the Oriental Orthodox and Roman Catholic Churches." (A revision of his paper presented in 1978.)
John Meno, "The Eucharistic Liturgy of the Syrian Orthodox Church."
Tiran Nersoyan, "Redemption Through the Blood of Christ."

---

[23]   Edited forms of those papers marked with an asterisk are included in this volume.

December 1979
Robert F. Taft, SJ, "The Liturgy of the Great Church: An Initial Synthesis of Structure and Interpretation on the Eve of Iconoclasm."

April 1980
Gabriel A. Abdelsayed, "The Coptic Orthodox Divine Liturgy: Some Texts and Their Use."

November 1980
Aidan Kavanagh, OSB, "The Eucharistic Liturgy of the Roman Catholic Church."
Edward J. Kilmartin, SJ, "Guidelines for the Oriental Orthodox and Roman Catholic Churches' Dialogue: Purpose, Scope, and Method of the Dialogue Between the Oriental Orthodox and Roman Catholic Churches." (A further revision of his paper presented in 1978 and 1979.)*

December 1981
Edward J. Kilmartin, SJ, "The Active Role of Christ and the Spirit in the Divine Liturgy."
K. M. Simon, "The Holy Spirit in the Sacraments of the Oriental Orthodox Churches"

September 1982
Gabriel A. Abdelsayed, "The Eucharistic Liturgies of the Coptic Orthodox Church: A Search for the Anamnesis and Epiclesis."
Aelred Cody, OSB, "Words of Institution, Words of Epiclesis in Western Thought and Practice."
Archbishop Yesehaq, "The Structure and Practice of the Ethiopian Church Liturgy."

April 1983
Arten Ashjian, "Intermarriage and the Armenian Church."
Edward J. Kilmartin, SJ, "Marriages Celebrated between a Roman Catholic and Non-Catholic Eastern Christian: Roman Catholic Legislation."

January 1984
Arten Ashjian and John Meno, "Mixed Marriages: Oriental Orthodox Pastoral Practice."
Sarhad Jammo, "The Chaldean Raze."

December 1984
Arten Ashjian, "An Armenian Orthodox Perception of the Establishing of Eastern Catholic Exarchates in the U.S.A."
Gabriel Duffy, "Roman Catholic and Oriental Orthodox Marriages."

December 1985
Aidan Kavanagh, OSB, "The Earliest Liturgies of Christian Baptism."
Garabed D. Kochakian, "Chrismation in the Oriental Orthodox Tradition."

1986
Robert Taft, SJ, ed., "The Oriental Orthodox Churches in the United States." (Published; see note 16 above.)

August 1988
Aelred Cody, OSB, "The Origins and First Ten Years of the Oriental Orthodox-Roman Catholic Consultation in the U.S.A."

June 1989
Garabed Kochakian, "The First Ten Years of Dialogue."
John Long, SJ, "The Four Vienna Consultations and the Roman Catholic Church."
John Long, SJ, "Oriental Orthodox-Roman Catholic Dialogue in the U.S.A."

February 1990
Thomas Bird and John Meno, eds., "A Compendium of Statements Made by Bishops of Rome and Oriental Orthodox Primates and Hierarchs."
Garabed Kochakian, "The Perception of the Roman Church by the Oriental Orthodox Churches."

September 1992
Garabed Kochakian and John Meno, "Guidelines for Oriental Orthodox/ Roman Catholic Marriages."
John Long, SJ, "Commentary on the Letter of Cardinals Willebrands and Philippe to the Coptic Catholic Patriarch and on the Principles Signed by Pope John Paul II and Pope Shenouda III in 1979."

June 1993
Garabed Kochakian and John Meno, "Guidelines for Oriental Orthodox/ Roman Catholic Marriages." (Revision of the paper presented in 1992.)*

Ronald G. Roberson, CSP, "The Contemporary Relationship Between the Catholic and Oriental Orthodox Churches." (Further revision of an essay first published as "The Modern Roman Catholic-Oriental Orthodox Dialogue," *One in Christ* 21 [1985] 238-254; then, with the first title, in *The Vienna Dialogue*, vol. 1, pp. 23-38.)*

May 1994

Garabed Kochakian and John Meno, "Guidelines for Oriental Orthodox/ Roman Catholic Marriages." (Further revision of the paper presented in 1992 and 1993.)

Frederick R. McManus, "Marriage in the Canons of the Eastern Catholic Churches."*

The Contemporary Relationship Between the Catholic and Oriental Orthodox Churches

by Reverend Ronald G. Roberson, CSP

Today the term "Oriental Orthodox Churches" generally refers to a communion of six independent ancient eastern Churches.[1] The common element among them is their non-reception of the christological teachings of the Council of Chalcedon, which was celebrated in 451.[2] These Churches are the Armenian Apostolic Church,[3] the Coptic Orthodox Church, the Ethiopian Orthodox Church, the Syrian Orthodox Church, and the Malankara Orthodox Syrian Church in India.[4] In addition, an independent Orthodox Church of Eritrea was established following that country's independence from Ethiopia in 1993. All are members of the World Council of Churches and have committed themselves to the contemporary ecumenical movement. In total, there are probably about thirty million Oriental Orthodox faithful in the world today.[5]

In the 1960s, these Churches began a process of rapprochement with both the Catholic and Orthodox[6] Churches. This paper examines the renewed relationship of the Oriental Orthodox Churches with the Catholic

---

[1] The Assyrian Church of the East, descended from the ancient East Syrian or "Nestorian" Church which rejected the christological teachings of the Council of Ephesus in 431, is not included in this study, although it is at times incorrectly referred to as one of the Oriental Orthodox Churches. Because of its christological tradition, the Assyrian Church is not in communion with any other Church.

[2] See W. de Vries, "The Reasons for the Rejection of the Council of Chalcedon by the Oriental Orthodox Churches," *Wort und Wahrheit,* Supplementary Issue No. 1 (Vienna: Herder, 1972) 54-60.

[3] The Armenian Apostolic Church is made up of two independent Catholicosates which are separate members of the World Council of Churches. The Catholicosate of Etchmiadzin, in the former Soviet republic of Armenia, is recognized as the first see. The Catholicosate of Cilicia is based at Antelias, Lebanon. In addition, two Armenian Patriarchates in Istanbul and Jerusalem are autonomous Churches dependent on Etchmiadzin.

[4] The Malankara Orthodox Syrian Church is autocephalous and includes about half of the total 2,000,000 Oriental Orthodox faithful in India. The other half makes up the autonomous Malankara Syrian Orthodox Church, which is dependent upon the Syrian Orthodox Patriarchate in Damascus.

[5] See membership statistics provided in Ans J. vander Bent, ed., *Handbook: Member Churches, World Council of Churches,* Fully Revised Edition (Geneva: World Council of Churches, 1985).

[6] I use the term "Orthodox" without the adjective "Oriental" to refer to the Orthodox Churches of the Byzantine tradition which are in communion with the Patriarch of Constantinople, whom they recognize as a point of unity. On relations between the Oriental Orthodox and Orthodox Churches, see André de Halleux, "Actualité du néochalcédonisme: Un accord christologique récent entre Orthodoxes," *Revue théologique de Louvain* 21 (1990) 32-54, and Paulos Gregorios, William Lazareth, Nikos Nissiotis, eds., *Does Chalcedon Divide or Unite? Towards Convergence in Orthodox Christology* (Geneva: World Council of Churches, 1981).

Church, which took place through unofficial theological consultations, visits between popes and hierarchs of these Churches, and official theological dialogues with the Coptic Orthodox and Malankara Orthodox Syrian Churches. The paper begins with a chronological presentation of the way in which the ancient christological dispute has been addressed and shows how major progress has been made as a result of the symbiotic relationship that developed between theologians meeting unofficially on the one hand, and church leaders meeting officially on the other. The second section focuses on ecclesiology, in which significant divergences remain to be resolved, despite the mutual recognition of each other as Churches.

1. Christology

The Oriental Orthodox said little about christology in their earliest encounters with Pope Paul VI. But the pope seems to have been convinced that the ancient disputes over christological terminology should no longer prevent the two Churches from professing their faith in Christ together.[7] In his welcoming speech to Armenian Catholicos Khoren I of Cilicia in May 1967, Pope Paul said:

> With you We give glory to the one God, Father, Son, and Holy Spirit; with you We acclaim Jesus Christ, Son of God, Incarnate Word, our Redeemer, the founder and head of the holy Church, his mystical body.[8]

During his visit to Armenian Patriarch of Constantinople Shnork Kalustian in July 1967, Pope Paul pointed out the importance of the Council of Ephesus' teaching as the basis of the unity of the two Churches:

> It is a great consolation to meditate upon the vision of Christ presented to the Church and to the world by that holy assembly. That vision, too, we share in common. God, made man for our salvation, is the God we confess in our Creed and preach to the world.[9]

---

[7] From the Catholic point of view, the idea that the dispute was essentially a question of terminology had been officially expressed as early as 1951, when Pope Pius XII stated in his encyclical *Sempiternus Rex* that these Christians "verbis praecipue a recto tramite deflectere videantur" ("seem to depart from the right path chiefly in words"). *Acta Apostolicae Sedis* 43 (1951) 636.

[8] *Acta Apostolicae Sedis* 59 (1967) 510.

[9] *Information Service* [Secretariat for Promoting Christian Unity] 3 (1967/3) 13.

And in his speech to Armenian Catholicos Vasken I (Etchmiadzin) in May 1970, Pope Paul stated that the different expressions of the one faith are due in large part to non-theological factors:

> If we have come to divergent expressions of the central mystery of our faith because of unfortunate circumstances, cultural differences and the difficulty of translating terms worked out with much effort and given precise statement only gradually, then research into these doctrinal difficulties must be undertaken again in order to understand what has brought them about and to be able to overcome them in a brotherly way.[10]

The pope went on to quote Nerses IV, a twelfth-century Armenian Catholicos, who wrote that the term "two natures" would be acceptable insofar as it indicates the absence of any confusion of humanity and divinity in Christ, against Eutyches and Apollinaris. Pope Paul then asked: "Has the time not come to clear up once and for all such misunderstandings inherited from the past?"[11]

In the *Common Declaration* signed at the end of Vasken's visit, both Churches made a clear commitment to encourage theological research into the remaining difficulties:

> They exhort theologians to devote themselves to a common study leading to a deepening of their understanding of the mystery of our Lord Jesus Christ and of the revelation brought about in him. . . . For their part, the Pope and the Catholicos will try to do all that is possible to support these efforts and will give them their pastoral blessing.[12]

The *Pro Oriente* foundation in Vienna took up this challenge and sponsored a historic series of discussions between theologians of the two communions. The first "Non-Official Ecumenical Consultation between Theologians of the Oriental Orthodox and the Roman Catholic Churches" took place in Vienna in September 1971. In the communiqué issued at the end of the meet-

---

[10] *Information Service* 11 (1970/III) 5-6.
[11] Ibid., 6.
[12] *Acta Apostolicae Sedis* 62 (1970) 116.

ing, the theologians affirmed that a common basis had been found in the apostolic traditions and the first three ecumenical councils. After rejecting both Eutychian and Nestorian christologies, they expressed their common faith in Christ in these words:

> We believe that our Lord and Saviour, Jesus Christ, is God the Son Incarnate; perfect in his divinity and perfect in his humanity. His divinity was not separated from his humanity for a single moment, not for the twinkling of an eye. His humanity is one with his divinity without commixtion, without confusion, without division, without separation. We in our common faith in the one Lord Jesus Christ, regard his mystery inexhaustible and ineffable and for the human mind never fully comprehensible or expressible.
>
> We see that there are still differences in the theological interpretation of the mystery of Christ because of our different ecclesiastical and theological traditions; we are convinced, however, that these differing formulations on both sides can be understood along the lines of the faith of Nicea and Ephesus.[13]

This text reveals an effort to avoid terminology which had been the focus of ancient disputes. Indeed, the words "person" and "nature" never appear. It is an effort to create a new vocabulary, using new concepts to express the one faith which underlies both traditional formulations.

The importance of this theological breakthrough was quickly realized. When the Syrian Patriarch Ignatius Yacoub III visited Rome one month later, Pope Paul was already echoing the findings of the *Pro Oriente* meeting when he said that theologians discussing the issue "are convinced . . . that these various formulations can be understood along the lines of the early councils, which is the faith we also profess."[14]

This thought was also reflected in the *Common Declaration*, which was signed at the end of the Patriarch's visit:

> Progress has already been made and Pope Paul VI and the Patriarch Mar Ignatius III are in agreement that there is

---

[13] "Communiqué," *Wort und Wahrheit*, Supplementary Issue No. 1 (Vienna: Herder, 1972) 182.

[14] *Information Service* 16 (1972/I) 3.

no difference in the faith they profess concerning the mystery of the Word of God made flesh and become really man, even if over the centuries difficulties have arisen out of the different theological expressions by which this faith was expressed.[15]

In May 1973 Coptic Pope[16] Shenouda III visited Pope Paul VI in Rome. The profession of faith contained in the *Common Declaration* they signed at the end of the meeting had clearly benefited from the *Pro Oriente* formulation:

> We confess that our Lord and God and Saviour and King of us all, Jesus Christ, is perfect God with respect to His divinity, perfect man with respect to His humanity. In Him His divinity is united with His humanity in a real, perfect union without mingling, without commixtion, without confusion, without alteration, without division, without separation. His divinity did not separate from His humanity for an instant, not for the twinkling of an eye. He who is God eternal and invisible became visible in the flesh, and took upon Himself the form of a servant. In Him are preserved all the properties of the divinity and all the properties of the humanity, together in a real, perfect, indivisible and inseparable union.[17]

Despite the historic nature of this joint christological declaration, the theologians involved in the *Pro Oriente* consultations realized that more progress could be made. Christology, then, still figured strongly in their discussions at the second meeting which took place in September 1973. In the final communiqué, the theologians of both communions built on what had been said in the 1971 statement. They added that the mystery of Christ is incomprehensible, and that all concepts about him are limited. Thus correct christological formulations can be wrongly understood, and behind an apparently wrong formulation there can be a right understanding. This fact en-

---

[15] *Acta Apostolicae Sedis* 63 (1971) 814.
[16] The Coptic Patriarchs of Alexandria have had the title "Pope" since ancient times. His full title is "Pope and Patriarch of the Great City of Alexandria and of all Egypt, the Middle East, Ethiopia, Nubia, and the Pentapolis."
[17] *Acta Apostolicae Sedis* 65 (1973) 300.

abled them to affirm that "the definition of the Council of Chalcedon, rightly understood today, affirms the unity of person and the indissoluble union of Godhead and Manhood in Christ despite the phrase 'in two natures.' "[18]

The statement also deals with problems of terminology:

> For those of us in the Western tradition, to hear of the one nature of Christ can be misleading, because it may be misunderstood as a denial of his humanity. For those of us in the Oriental Orthodox Churches to hear of two natures can be misleading because it can be misunderstood as affirming two persons in Christ. But both sides agree in rejecting Eutychianism and Nestorianism. . . .
>
> Our common effort to clarify the meaning of the Greek terms *hypostasis* and *physis* in the trinitarian and christological contexts made us realize how difficult it was to find a satisfactory definition of these terms that could do justice to both contexts in a consistent manner.[19]

The communiqué also calls for new terminology which would express more effectively the mystery of Christ for people today.

Since 1973, popes and heads of Oriental Orthodox Churches have affirmed repeatedly that they share the same faith in Christ, an assumption taken for granted in most of their statements. For instance, during his visit to Rome in June 1983, Moran Mar Baselius Marthoma Mathews I, the Catholicos of the Malankara Orthodox Syrian Church of India, quoted Cyril of Alexandria's "one divine-human nature" formula as being part of the common faith of the two Churches.[20]

Another significant christological text was issued in June 1984, at the conclusion of the visit of Syrian Orthodox Patriarch Ignatius Zakka I Iwas to Rome. The pope and patriarch maintained in their *Common Declaration* that past schisms "in no way affect or touch the substance of their faith," since the divisions arose from terminological misunderstandings. They then made the following joint confession of faith in the mystery of the Word made flesh:

> In our turn we confess that He became incarnate for us, taking to himself a real body with a rational soul. He shared

---

[18] "Communiqué," *Wort und Wahrheit*, Supplementary Issue No. 2 (Vienna: Herder, 1974) 175-176.
[19] Ibid., 176.
[20] *Information Service* 52 (1983/III) 74.

our humanity in all things but sin. We confess that our
Lord and our God, our Saviour and the King of all, Jesus
Christ, is perfect God as to His divinity and perfect man
as to His humanity. This Union is real, perfect, without
blending or mingling, without confusion, without alteration, without division, without the least separation. He
who is God eternal and invisible, became visible in the
flesh and took the form of servant. In Him are united, in a
real, perfect indivisible and inseparable way, divinity and
humanity, and in Him all their properties are present and
active.[21]

Catholic and Coptic representatives meeting at Amba Bishoy monastery in February 1988 reaffirmed the christological agreement with the Coptic
Orthodox Church. They also adopted this more concise formulation which was
intended to make the christological accord more accessible to the faithful:

We believe that our Lord, God and Saviour Jesus Christ,
the Incarnate–Logos, is perfect in His Divinity and perfect in His Humanity. He made His Humanity One with
His Divinity without Mixture, nor Mingling, nor Confusion. His Divinity was not separated from His Humanity
even for a moment or twinkling of an eye. At the same
time, we Anathematize the Doctrines of both Nestorius
and Eutyches.[22]

This progress on christology was noted with satisfaction by the participants at the fifth *Pro Oriente* consultation in September 1988. They went on
to emphasize the following:

. . . that the great mystery of the Incarnation of the Son of
God could not be exhaustively formulated in words, and
that within the limits of condemned errors like Arianism,
Nestorianism and Eutychianism, a certain plurality of expressions was permissible in relation to the inseparable and
unconfused hypostatic unity of the human and the divine

---

[21]   *Information Service* 55 (1984/II-III) 62.
[22]   *Information Service* 69 (1989/1) 8.

> in one Lord Jesus Christ, the Word of God incarnate by
> the Holy Spirit of the Blessed Virgin Mary, consubstantial
> with God the Father in His divinity and consubstantial
> with us in his humanity.[23]

Another christological agreement was reached at the first meeting of the new Joint International Commission for Dialogue between the Roman Catholic Church and the Malankara Syrian Orthodox Church of India, held at Kottayam in October 1989.[24] The statement was officially approved by the authorities of both Churches and published on June 3, 1990. It includes this text on the relationship between Christ's humanity and divinity in paragraph 5:

> Our Lord Jesus Christ is one, perfect in his humanity and
> perfect in his divinity, at once consubstantial with the Fa-
> ther in his divinity, and consubstantial with us in his hu-
> manity. His humanity is one with his divinity—without
> change, without commingling, without division and with-
> out separation. In the Person of the Eternal Logos Incar-
> nate are united and active in a real and perfect way the
> divine and human natures, with all their properties, facul-
> ties and operations.[25]

This put an end to any christological disagreement between the Catholic and Malankara Orthodox Syrian Churches.

A careful reading of the statements issued over the past twenty-five years indicates that the ancient christological dispute between the Oriental Orthodox Churches and the Catholic Church has been substantially resolved. Even though different interpretations of the meaning of the Chalcedonian definition remain, the Churches have been able to set aside the old disputes and affirm that their faith in the mystery of Christ which transcends all formulations is, in fact, the same.

2. Ecclesiology

Progress has also been made in the area of ecclesiology, although certain differences remain to be resolved. The nature of an ecumenical council has

---

[23]   "Communiqué," *Wort und Wahrheit*, Supplementary Issue No. 5 (Vienna: Herder, 1989) 149.

[24]   See G. Daucourt, "First meeting for dialogue with Syrian Orthodox Church of India," *L'Osservatore Romano*, English weekly edition, November 27, 1989, 2.

[25]   *L'Osservatore Romano*, June 3, 1990, 5.

figured prominently in the theological discussion, since the Oriental Orthodox have received only the first three of the seven ancient councils accepted
by the Catholic and Orthodox Churches. The concept and exercise of primacy is another area of disagreement, especially since the Oriental Orthodox
have no experience of primacy among their five independent Churches. Not
even a limited form of primacy exists similar to the role that the Patriarchate
of Constantinople plays among the Orthodox Churches. A third sensitive
area is the existence of the Eastern Catholic Churches and the related question of proselytism between members of the two communions.

Before examining these areas of disparity, it is necessary to review the
way both Churches have consistently stated their recognition of the ecclesial
reality of the other. Statements of this type are found at the very beginning of
the series of visits between popes and Oriental Orthodox hierarchs. In May
1970, when Catholicos Vasken I visited Pope Paul VI, he said, "We have
remembered, as in a reawakening, that we have been brothers for the past
two thousand years."[26] Paul VI responded:

> Let us give thanks to the Lord together that day by day
> the profound sacramental reality existing between our
> Churches is made known to us, beyond the daily differ-
> ences and the hostilities of the past.[27]

And in their *Common Declaration* at the conclusion of the visit, the
two church leaders affirmed that collaboration and research "must be founded
on reciprocal recognition of the Christian faith and of common sacramental
life, on mutual respect of persons and of their Churches."[28]

The *Common Declaration* of Paul VI and Coptic Pope Shenouda III in
May 1973 stated that Catholics and Copts are rediscovering each other as
Churches despite the divisions of the past:

> These differences cannot be ignored. In spite of them,
> however, we are rediscovering ourselves as Churches with
> a common inheritance and are reaching out with deter-
> mination and confidence in the Lord to achieve the full-
> ness and perfection of that unity which is His gift.[29]

---

[26] *Information Service* 11 (1970/III) 9.
[27] Ibid.
[28] *Acta Apostolicae Sedis* 62 (1970) 416.
[29] *Acta Apostolicae Sedis* 65 (1973) 300-301.

During his visit to Istanbul in 1979, John Paul II spoke to Armenian Patriarch Shnork of "the unity which already exists between us." And in response, Patriarch Shnork indicated that both are parts of the one Church:

> Such visits serve the praiseworthy purpose of deepening the love, respect, and mutual understanding between various parts of the Christian Church. We shall always pray that God may bless this renewal of relations, which is manifested through such visits.[30]

This recognition of the full ecclesial reality of both Churches has been stated repeatedly during subsequent visits and in common declarations. For instance, in 1981 John Paul II made the following statement to Ethiopian Orthodox Patriarch Tekle Haimanot:

> The contacts which we have reestablished are now enabling us to rediscover the profound and true reality of this existing unity. Even the real divergences between us are being seen more clearly as we gradually free them from so many secondary elements that derive from ambiguities of language.[31]

In later pronouncements, John Paul II and heads of Oriental Orthodox Churches have listed areas of cooperation which this rediscovered relationship makes possible. The *Joint Communiqué* issued at the end of the visit to Rome of Armenian Catholicos Karekin II of Cilicia in April 1983 encouraged cooperation in the theological formation of clerics and laity, catechetical instruction, practical solutions of situations of common pastoral concern, social action, cultural promotion, and humanitarian services.[32]

In their *Common Declaration* (June 1984), Pope John Paul II and Patriarch Ignatius Zakka I Iwas considered the two Churches so close that they even envisaged cooperation in pastoral care, including some sacramental sharing:

> It is not rare, in fact, for our faithful to find access to a priest of their own Church materially or morally impos-

---

[30] *Information Service* 41 (1979/IV) 28.
[31] *Information Service* 47 (1981/III-IV) 100.
[32] *Information Service* 51 (1983/I-II) 40.

sible. Anxious to meet their needs and with their spiritual benefit in mind, we authorize them in such cases to
ask for the sacraments of penance, Eucharist, and anointing of the sick from lawful priests of either of our two
sister Churches, when they need them.[33]

The historic nature of this declaration goes without saying. It is the
first time in modern history that the Catholic Church and a Church separated from it have agreed to allow some forms of sacramental sharing.

In addition, the same declaration envisages cooperation in the formation and education of clergy:

It would be a logical corollary of collaboration in pastoral
care to cooperate in priestly formation and theological
education. Bishops are encouraged to promote sharing of
facilities for theological education where they judge it to
be advisable.[34]

All this was made possible because of the pope and patriarch's common wish:

. . . to widen the horizon of their brotherhood and affirm
herewith the terms of the deep spiritual communion which
already unites them and the prelates, clergy, and faithful
of both their Churches, to consolidate these ties of Faith,
Hope, and Love, and to advance in finding a wholly common ecclesial life.[35]

Recent speeches and common declarations now frequently state that
what unites the Churches is far greater than what divides them; these communications also list common elements such as belief in the Trinity, the mystery of Christ, the apostolic traditions, the sacraments, the Theotokos, and
especially the first three ecumenical councils.

In spite of all this, important areas of disagreement remain. Participants at the second *Pro Oriente* theological consultation in 1973 considered

---

[33]   *Information Service* 55 (1984/II-III) 63.
[34]   Ibid.
[35]   Ibid., 62.

ecclesiological questions for the first time, and the third and fourth meetings were devoted entirely to this area. Ecclesiological issues also figured prominently at the fifth meeting.

The communiqué of the second consultation treated the question of ecumenical councils and the relationship between the papacy and councils in a tentative way. The members agreed that the first three councils have a "greater degree of fullness" because of their wider acceptance by Christians. Moreover, they "look forward to future regional and ecumenical councils with larger representation as the reunion of Churches is hastened by the working of the Holy Spirit." On the relationship between Pope and Council, they praised the notion of collegiality expressed in the documents of Vatican II as "a move in the right direction according to which the role of the bishop of Rome is seen within the Council and not above it."[36]

The theologians were able to reach greater consensus on these issues in 1976 at the third *Pro Oriente* meeting. The communiqué described areas of agreement on the nature of the Church and the notion of conciliarity. The text begins by affirming that unity is Christ's gift to the Church. This is a unity which allows for a "multiplicity of traditions," in which "diversity has to be held together by basic unity in fundamental matters."

The communiqué goes on to speak of the identity of the local and universal Churches:

> One and the same Church, for there cannot be more than one, is manifested both locally and universally as a koinonia of truth and love, characterized by eucharistic communion and the corporate unity of the episcopate. The unity of the Church has its source and prototype in the unity of the Father, the Son and the Holy Spirit, into which we have been baptized.[37]

Conciliarity is described as the following:

> . . . the understanding of the Church as koinonia, so essential to the nature of the Church as the Body of Christ, and so clearly visible in the structure of its life and leadership from the very inception.[38]

---

[36] "Communiqué," *Wort und Wahrheit,* Supplementary Issue No. 2 (Vienna: Herder, 1974) 176.
[37] "Communiqué," *Wort und Wahrheit,* Supplementary Issue No. 3 (Vienna: Herder, 1976) 223.
[38] Ibid.

The communiqué considers the council or synod both as a single event and as a continuing structure of the Church's life. Insofar as it is an event, the theologians stated:

> [We] could not agree on how and by whom such a world-wide council of our Churches should be convoked and conducted, nor could we agree completely on the procedure for the reception of past or future councils.[39]

Nevertheless, they agreed that Churches have the right to convoke a council in this manner:

> . . . whenever found necessary and possible though there is no necessity to hold ecumenical councils at given intervals as a permanent structure of the Church. We recognize the need of structures of coordination between the autocephalous Churches for the settlement of disputes and for facing together the problems and tasks confronting our Churches in the modern world.[40]

The question of councils was taken up again in the communiqué issued by the fifth consultation in 1988. It reaffirms that the first three ecumenical councils provided the basis for the common faith of Catholics and Oriental Orthodox and acknowledged that the Oriental Orthodox are "not in a position formally to accept" the Council of Chalcedon and the ones following it. However, further study of the later councils was recommended. The communiqué also examined the nature of the reception of conciliar teaching and recognized it as a complex process that sometimes does not include formal reception of conciliar decisions as such.[41]

The fourth consultation (September 1978) discussed two more problems which divide the Catholic and Oriental Orthodox Churches: the notion of primacy and the status of Eastern Catholic Churches. Primacy was taken up again at the fifth meeting.

The communiqué of the fourth consultation describes primacy in the context of what it calls three integrally related elements in the life of the Church: primacy, conciliarity, and the consensus of the believing commu-

---

[39]   Ibid.
[40]   Ibid., 223-224.
[41]   "Communiqué," *Wort und Wahrheit*, Supplementary Issue Number 5 (Vienna: Herder, 1989) 149-150.

nity. It recognizes, however, that "their relative importance has been differently understood in different situations."

The Oriental Orthodox understand primacy as being "of historical and ecclesiological origin," while Catholics see it as part of "the divine plan for the Church." Yet both sides acknowledge that primacy is connected with the continuing guidance of the Holy Spirit within the Church. The Catholic teachings about the primacy of the bishop of Rome "are to be understood in the context of their historical, sociological and political conditions and also in the light of the historical evolution of the whole teaching of the Roman Church, a process which is still continuing."[42]

The Oriental Orthodox, on the other hand, "have not felt it necessary to formulate verbally and declare their understanding of primacy though it is clearly implied in the continuing life and teaching of their Churches."[43]

The consultation called for more research and reflection on primacy "with a new vision for our future unity."

With regard to infallibility, both sides affirmed that it "pertains to the Church as a whole." But they could not agree on "the relative importance of different organs in the Church through which this inerrant teaching authority is to find expression."

The participants stated that Catholics and Oriental Orthodox should strive toward the following goal:

> . . . full union of sister Churches—with communion in the faith, in the sacraments of the Church, in ministry and within a canonical structure. Each Church as well as all Churches together will have a primatial and conciliar structure, providing for their communion in a given place as well as on regional and worldwide scale.[44]

The statement goes on to address the focus of such communion and the role that Rome might play in it:

> The structure will be basically conciliar. No single Church in this communion will by itself be regarded as the source and origin of that communion; the source of the unity of the Church is the action of the triune God, Father, Son

---

[42] "Communiqué," *Wort und Wahrheit*, Supplementary Issue Number 4 (Vienna: Herder, 1978) 233.
[43] Ibid.
[44] Ibid.

and Holy Spirit. It is the same Spirit who operates in all sister Churches the same faith, hope and love, as well as ministry and sacraments. About regarding one particular Church as the center of the unity, there was no agreement, though the need of a special ministry for unity was recognized by all.

This communion will find diverse means of expression—the exchange of letters of peace among the Churches, the public liturgical remembering of the Churches and their primates by each other, the placing of responsibility for convoking general synods in order to deal with common concerns of the Churches, and so on.[45]

At the fifth consultation in 1988 the members recognized that both the Catholic and Oriental Orthodox Churches possess some form of primacy, always related to the conciliar nature of the Church. In the Catholic Church the Bishop of Rome's primacy serves the unity of all the Churches; the Oriental Orthodox experience primacy *within* each of their five independent Churches, not at a level above them. Members of the consultation recommended further study of this question and acknowledged that in practice some form of both central coordination and local autonomy was needed.[46]

This lack of full agreement on the function of conciliarity and primacy within the Church explains why these topics are almost never mentioned in the speeches and common declarations issued as a result of visits between popes and heads of Oriental Orthodox Churches. The 1973 *Common Declaration* of Pope Paul VI and Pope Shenouda III contains the broad sentence, "We have, to a large degree, the same understanding of the Church, founded upon the Apostles, and of the important role of ecumenical and local councils."[47] The fact that nothing more specific could be said indicates the continuing divergence in the two Churches' understanding of this important area in ecclesial life. In fact, after the 1973 meeting between Paul VI and Shenouda III, there were no visits between a pope and the head of an Oriental Orthodox Church for six years. The next contact occurred when a Coptic Orthodox delegation visited John Paul II in 1979. The delegation carried a letter to John Paul in which Shenouda expressed his concern about the lack of progress in the area of ecclesiology.

---

[45]   Ibid.

[46]   "Communiqué," *Wort und Wahrheit*, Supplementary Issue Number 5, (Vienna: Herder, 1989) 150.

[47]   *Acta Apostolicae Sedis* 65 (1973) 300.

The 1973 *Common Declaration* set up a special Joint Commission between the Catholic and Coptic Orthodox Churches to "guide common study in the fields of Church tradition, patristics, liturgy, theology, history and practical problems, so that by cooperation in common we may seek to resolve, in a spirit of mutual respect, the differences existing between our Churches."[48] By 1979, this commission had met four times in Cairo[49] and continued to make progress in the area of christology but not ecclesiology, as Pope Shenouda wrote in his letter to John Paul:

> In ecclesiology only very little real progress has been reached. This is why we thought it appropriate to delegate an official delegation of six members of the official Commission, in order to enhance the negotiations between our two Churches, which seem to have stopped at a point without reaching further steps of real progress in the achievement of the unity of our two Churches.[50]

In his speech to the delegation, Pope John Paul responded to some concerns raised in Pope Shenouda's letter. Although he did not address the question of conciliarity, he did speak on the role of the papacy in the dialogue:

> I know that one of the fundamental questions of the ecumenical movement is the nature of that full communion we are seeking with each other and the role that the Bishop of Rome has to play, by God's design, in serving that communion of faith and spiritual life, which is nourished by the sacraments and expressed in fraternal charity. A great deal of progress has been made in deepening our understanding of this question. Much remains to be done. I consider your visit to me and to the See of Rome a significant contribution towards resolving this question definitively.[51]

---

[48] Ibid., 301.

[49] See reports on these meetings in *Proche Orient Chrétien*: "La commission mixte de l'Église copte orthodoxe et de l'Église catholique," 24 (1974) 68-69; "Première réunion de la commission mixte des Églises catholique et copte orthodoxe," 24 (1974) 175-178; "Deuxième réunion de la commission mixte," 25 (1975) 314-316; "[Troisième] Réunion de la commission mixte," 26 (1976) 360-361; "[Quatrième] Réunion de la commission mixte," 29 (1979) 107-109.

[50] *Information Services* 41 (1979/IV) 8.

[51] Ibid., 7.

One could raise a question about how Pope John Paul understood the visit of the Coptic delegation to Rome as "a significant contribution towards resolving this question definitively." Perhaps this statement gives an example of the kind of communion he would envisage taking place after the reestablishment of unity: occasional official visits between heads of sister Churches to inform the universal primate about the lives of their Churches, or the type of communion outlined in the fourth *Pro Oriente* communiqué.

In the same speech, Pope John Paul emphasized that the re-establishment of communion between the Churches would not imply a loss of the identity of either of them:

> Fundamental to this dialogue is the recognition that the richness of this unity in faith and spiritual life has to be expressed in diversity of forms. Unity—whether on the universal level or the local level—does not mean uniformity or absorption of one group by another. It is rather at the service of all groups to help each live better the proper gifts it has received from God's Spirit. . . . With no one trying to dominate each other but to serve each other, all together will grow into that perfection of unity for which Our Lord prayed on the night before he died.[52]

Unfortunately, the political situation in Egypt worsened soon after this visit, and Pope Shenouda was placed under house arrest by President Sadat in September 1981. This brought the dialogue between the Catholic and Coptic Orthodox Churches to a virtual standstill. It was only after Pope Shenouda's release in January 1985 that the commission could resume its work.[53]

---

[52] Ibid.

[53] The first phase of the commission's work was concluded with the adoption of a brief christological statement in 1988. The second phase, which was to examine other issues, began with the commission's fifth meeting at Amba Bishoy monastery in October 1988. The discussion at this meeting centered on the mystery of the redemption and the final destiny of the human person. See report in *Irénikon* 61 (1988) 537-539, *Information Service* 68 (1988/III-IV) 164, and *Proche Orient Chrétien* 39 (1989) 330-333. The sixth session, which took place at the same monastery in April 1990, discussed the procession of the Holy Spirit and the *filioque*. See *Proche Orient Chrétien* 40 (1990) 301-303, and *Irénikon* 63 (1990) 213-215. The seventh session, held in April 1991, studied the situation of the faithful after death and the Catholic teaching on purgatory. It also set up a joint pastoral commission to deal with concrete local problems involving the faithful of the two communities. See *Irénikon* 64 (1991) 236-237, and *Proche Orient Chrétien* 41 (1991) 362-364. The discussion continued at the eighth meeting in February 1992: *Irénikon* 65 (1992) 63-65. The ninth meeting, scheduled for April 1993, had to be canceled because of technical difficulties.

In their *Common Declaration* of June 1984, Pope John Paul II and Syrian Patriarch Ignatius Zakka I Iwas added significant new elements to the developing ecclesiological consensus between the two Churches. This declaration draws from the work of other interconfessional dialogues, and it places the Eucharist at the center of its understanding of the Church. Here the Eucharist is shown to be much more than one of the seven sacraments that Catholics and Syrian Orthodox have in common:

> Sacramental life finds in the holy Eucharist its fulfillment and its summit, in such a way that it is through the Eucharist that the Church most profoundly realizes and reveals its nature. . . . The other Sacraments . . . are ordered to that celebration of the holy Eucharist which is the centre of sacramental life and the chief visible expression of ecclesial communion. This communion of Christians with each other and of local Churches united around their lawful Bishops is realized in the gathered community which confesses the same faith.[54]

This is the first time that a common declaration makes such a connection between Church, Eucharist, and bishop. It represents an ecclesiological advance which needs to be amplified in future statements.

Another question concerning relations between Catholics and Oriental Orthodox focuses on the Eastern Catholic Churches. Until recently, Rome has presented its relationship with the Eastern Catholic Churches as a model for the relationship that should exist between the Catholic Church and any eastern Church that might come into communion with it.[55] The Oriental Orthodox, however, often take great offense at the very existence of these Churches, which are frequently the direct result of Catholic missionary activity among the Oriental Orthodox faithful. They see in this a denial of the ecclesial reality of the Oriental Orthodox Churches by the Catholic Church and claim that some Eastern Catholics continue to proselytize even now among the Oriental Orthodox faithful.

---

[54] *Information Service* 55 (1984/II-III) 62.

[55] See letter of Cardinal Willebrands to Russian Orthodox Metropolitan Juvenaly of September 22, 1979, where, in the context of a misunderstanding about a papal statement on the status of the Ukrainian Catholic Church, the Cardinal wrote, "There was no intention whatever of presenting the Union of Brest as the model for our relations with the Orthodox Churches today or as one for the contemplated future union." Text in T. Stransky and J. Sheerin, *Doing the Truth in Charity* (Ramsey: Paulist, 1982) 228.

The first mention of the Eastern Catholic Churches in encounters between popes and Oriental Orthodox hierarchs is found in the speech Paul VI delivered in the presence of Armenian Catholicos of Cilicia Khoren I in May 1967. Perhaps not attuned to Oriental Orthodox sensitivities in this matter, the pope expressed his affection for the Armenian tradition by recalling the *Decree for the Armenians* of the Council of Florence, the foundation of the Armenian College in Rome, the Armenian Catholic presence in Venice, and highly placed Armenian Catholics in the Roman Curia.[56] He made similar references in a speech during the visit of Catholicos Vasken I of Etchmiadzin in 1970.[57]

Oriental Orthodox concern about the activity of Eastern Catholics was mentioned indirectly in the *Common Declaration* of Paul VI and Shenouda III in 1973, which rejected all forms of proselytism as incompatible with the relationship that should exist between the two Churches:

> . . . We reject all forms of proselytism, in the sense of acts by which persons seek to disturb each other's communities by recruiting new members from each other through methods, or because of attitudes of mind, which are opposed to the exigencies of Christian love or to what should characterize the relationships between Churches. Let it cease, where it may exist.[58]

This statement was a response to Pope Shenouda's complaint that Coptic Catholics were proselytizing among Coptic Orthodox in Egypt. The Coptic Catholic Patriarch was reminded of this statement in a letter from Pope Paul soon thereafter.[59]

This issue has not been taken up in any of the speeches and common declarations since 1973. However, the fourth *Pro Oriente* meeting of 1978 made the following statement:

> The Oriental Catholic Churches will not even in the transitional period before full unity be regarded as a device for bringing Oriental Orthodox Churches inside the Roman communion. Their role will be more in terms of collaborating in the restoration of eucharistic communion among

---

[56] *Acta Apostolicae Sedis* 59 (1967) 511-512.
[57] *Information Service* 11 (1970/III) 5.
[58] *Acta Apostolicae Sedis* 65 (1973) 301.
[59] "Lettre du Pape Paul VI au Patriarche copte catholique," *Proche Orient Chrétien* 24 (1974) 351-354.

the sister Churches. The Oriental Orthodox Churches, according to the principles of Vatican II and subsequent statements of the See of Rome, cannot be fields of mission for other Churches. The sister Churches will work out lo-cal solutions, in accordance with differing local situations, implementing as far as possible the principle of a unified episcopate for each locality.[60]

The position of the Catholic Church which emerges from these state-ments is twofold. While it affirms the right of the Eastern Catholic Churches to exist, it also gives assurances that Catholics are not to proselytize among Oriental Orthodox Christians. Even so, many Oriental Orthodox remain suspicious of the true intentions of their Eastern Catholic counterparts and continue to feel that these Churches are made up of their own faithful who have been unjustly taken away from them.

The contemporary relationship between the Catholic and Oriental Orthodox Churches is unique, and the resolution of the christological di-vergences between the two communions is unprecedented. In no other ecu-menical relationship has a dogmatic disagreement of this type been overcome so unequivocally, and with such official approbation. This was achieved with-out any official bilateral dialogue taking place.[61] The interplay of unofficial theological consultations and official pronouncements made by Church lead-ers proved to be an effective means of resolving a centuries-old problem.

At the same time, the lack of any clearly defined ministry serving the unity of the various Oriental Orthodox Churches has necessitated a rather piecemeal process by which levels of agreement with individual Churches differ. The lack of a specific christological accord with the Armenian or Ethio-pian Churches somewhat relativizes the importance of the accord reached with the Copts, Syrians, and Malankaras. Nevertheless, progress has been substantial and provides real hope for the future.

Ecclesiology remains the area of greatest disagreement. It is doubtful that any of the Oriental Orthodox Churches will accept a form of unity with the Catholic Church that does not fully respect their administrative indepen-

---

[60] "Communiqué," *Wort und Wahrheit* Supplementary Issue No. 4 (Vienna: Herder, 1978) 233-234.

[61] It should be noted that the fifth *Pro Oriente* consultation in 1988 "urgently appeals to all the Churches represented here to set up a joint official body to engage in that formal dialogue between the Roman Catholic Church and the family of the Oriental Orthodox Churches which will have as its objective the achieving of full communion in faith and sacramental life." See text in *Wort und Wahrheit*, Supple-mentary Issue No. 5 (Vienna: Herder, 1989) 151.

dence. And the Catholic Church must decide if full communion with another Church necessarily means that the Bishop of Rome must have unlimited authority to intervene in the affairs of the other Church. These issues will provide ample material for research and reflection in the years to come as the relationship between these Churches reaches greater maturity. ⌒

APPENDIX

Official Visits: Popes and Oriental Orthodox Hierarchs

1. Armenian Catholicos Khoren I to Paul VI in Rome, May 9, 1967
   Two Speeches
   Acta Apostolicae Sedis 59 (1967) 510-512
   L'Osservatore Romano (May 10, 1967) 1

2. Paul VI to Patriarch Shnork Kalustian in Istanbul, July 25-26, 1967
   Two Speeches
   Information Service (1967/III) 13-14

3. Armenian Catholicos Vasken I to Paul VI in Rome, May 8-12, 1970
   a) Four Speeches
   Information Service 11 (1970/III) 3-10
   b) Common Declaration
   Acta Apostolicae Sedis 62 (1970) 416-417

First Pro Oriente *Theological Consultation: Vienna, September 7-12, 1971*

4. Syrian Patriarch Ignatius Yacoub III to Paul VI in Rome, October 25-27, 1971
   a) Four Speeches
   Information Service 16 (1972/I) 3-5
   b) Common Declaration
   Acta Apostolicae Sedis 63 (1971) 814-815

5. Coptic Pope Shenouda III to Paul VI in Rome, May 4-10, 1973
   a) Eight Speeches
   Information Service 22 (1973/IV) 3-10
   b) Common Declaration
   Acta Apostolicae Sedis 65 (1973) 299-301

Second Pro Oriente *Theological Consultation: Vienna, September 3-9, 1973*

Third Pro Oriente *Theological Consultation: Vienna, August 30 to September 5, 1976*

Fourth Pro Oriente *Theological Consultation: Vienna, September 11-17, 1978*

6. Reception of Coptic Delegation by John Paul II in Rome, June 23, 1979
   a) Letter from Pope Shenouda
   b) Speech by John Paul II
   Information Service 41 (1979/IV) 6-8

7. John Paul II to Armenian Patriarch Shnork in Istanbul, November 29, 1979
   Two Speeches
   Information Service 41 (1979/IV) 28-29

8. Syrian Patriarch Ignatius Yacoub III to John Paul II in Rome, May 13-16, 1980
   Four Speeches
   Information Service 44 (1980/III-IV) 92-95

9. Reception of Ethiopian Orthodox Delegation by John Paul II, July 16-19, 1980
   Two Letters
   Information Service 44 (1980/III-IV) 97-98

10. Ethiopian Patriarch Tekle Haimanot to John Paul II in Rome, October 17, 1981
    Two Speeches
    Information Service 47 (1981/III-IV) 100-101

11. Armenian Catholicos Karekin II to John Paul II in Rome, April 15-19, 1983
    a) Two Speeches
    b) Joint Communiqué
    Information Service 51 (1983/I-II) 37-41

12. Syrian Catholicos of India Moran Mar Baselius Marthoma Mathews I to John Paul II in Rome, June 2-5, 1983
    Two Speeches
    Information Service 52 (1983/III) 72-75

13. Syrian Patriarch Ignatius Zakka I Iwas to John Paul II in Rome, June 20-23, 1984
    a) Two Speeches
    b) Common Declaration
    Information Service 55 (1984/II-III) 59-63

14. John Paul II to Mar Basileus Paulos II, Catholicos of the Malankara Jacobite Syrian Orthodox Church in Kottayam, India, February 7, 1986
    Speech of John Paul II
    Information Service 60 (1986/I-II) 12-13

15. John Paul II to Syrian Catholicos of India Moran Mar Baselius Marthoma Mathews I in Kottayam, India, February 8, 1986
    a) Speech of John Paul II
    Information Service 60 (1986/I-II) 13-14
    Star of the East 8 (1986) 8-9
    b) Speech of Catholicos Marthoma Mathews I
    Star of the East 8 (1986) 5-7

Fifth Pro Oriente *Theological Consultation: Vienna, September 18-25, 1988*

16. Ethiopian Patriarch Abuna Paulos to John Paul II in Rome, June 11, 1993
    a) Speech of John Paul II
    L'Osservatore Romano (June 11-12, 1993) 4

The Common Declarations Signed by the Heads of the Roman Catholic and Oriental Orthodox Churches

I. The Common Declaration of Pope Paul VI and Armenian Orthodox Catholicos Vasken I: Rome, May 12,1970[1]

Paul VI, Bishop of Rome, Pope of the Catholic Church, and Vasken I, Supreme Catholicos-Patriarch of all Armenians, thank the Lord for having permitted them to pray together, to meet each other, and to exchange the holy kiss of peace, especially during this period of preparation for the great feast celebrating the Descent of the Holy Spirit upon the Apostles.

Conscious of their duties as pastors, they invite all Christians, especially those of the Catholic Church and the apostolic Armenian Church, to respond with greater fidelity to the call of the Holy Spirit stimulating them to a more profound unity, which will accomplish the will of our common Saviour and will render fruitful the service of the world by Christians.

This unity cannot be realized unless everyone, pastors and faithful, really strive to know each other. To this end, they urge theologians to apply themselves to a common study directed towards a more profound knowledge of the mystery of Our Lord Jesus Christ and revelation made in him. Faithful to the tradition handed down by the Apostles and the Fathers and at the same time aware of the demands of a world seeking God in the new developments of our age, they will be able to open up new avenues which will overcome the differences that still exist and bring their Churches to a more perfect unity in the profession of their faith in the face of the world. On their part, the Pope and the Catholicos will strive to do all they possibly can to support these efforts and give them their pastoral blessing.

However, the efforts run the risk of remaining sterile unless they are rooted in the whole life of the entire Church. This is why they hope that a closer collaboration will develop in all possible domains of the Christian life. Prayer in common, mutual spiritual aid, joint efforts to find really Christian solutions to the problems of the world today will be precious means in the service of this search for a full unity so greatly desired.

---

[1]   Taken from the compendium of documents presented by Professor Thomas Bird and Rt. Rev. John Meno at the February 1990 meeting of the consultation. French original: *Acta Apostolicae Sedis* 62 (1970) 416-417.

This search accomplished together, this collaboration must be based on the mutual recognition of the common Christian faith and the sacramental life, on the mutual respect of persons and their Churches. If the unselfish efforts they wish to foster wholeheartedly are inspired with this spirit and implemented in this manner, then they are confident that the spirit of truth and love will give to the members of the Catholic Church and the apostolic Armenian Church this truly Christian fraternity which is the fruit of his action in them.

In the name of this fraternity, Pope Paul VI and the Catholicos Vasken I raise their voices in solemn appeal to all those who exert influence on the life of nations and peoples so that they may strive to seek and to find all possible means to end wars, hatred, moral and physical violence, any oppression whatsoever of man by man. May the One who is our peace grant that this appeal be heard.

II. The Common Declaration of Pope Paul VI and Syrian Orthodox Patriarch Mar Ignatius Jacob III: Rome, October 27, 1971[2]

As they conclude their solemn meeting which marks a new step in the relations between the Roman Catholic Church and the Syrian Orthodox Church, His Holiness Pope Paul VI and His Holiness Mar Ignatius Jacob III humbly render thanks to Almighty God for having made possible this historic opportunity to pray together, to engage in a fraternal exchange of views concerning the needs of the Church of God, and to witness to their common desire that all Christians may intensify their service to the world with humility and complete dedication.

The Pope and the Patriarch have recognized the deep spiritual communion, which already exists between their Churches. The celebration of the sacraments of the Lord, the common profession of faith in the Lord Jesus Christ, the Word of God made man for man's salvation, the apostolic traditions which form part of the common heritage of both Churches, the great Fathers and Doctors, including St. Cyril of Alexandria, who are their common masters in the faith—all these testify to the action of the Holy Spirit, who has continued to work in their Churches even when there have been human weakness and failings. The period of mutual recrimination and condemnation has given place to a willingness to meet together in sincere efforts to lighten and eventually remove the burden of history, which still weighs heavily upon Christians.

Progress has already been made, and Pope Paul VI and the Patriarch Mar Ignatius Jacob III are in agreement that there is no difference in the faith

---

[2] Signed by the Pope and Patriarch in the presence of the Synod Bishops. English original: *Acta Apostolicae Sedis* 63 (1971) 814-815.

they profess concerning the mystery of the Word of God made flesh and be-come really man, even if over the centuries difficulties have arisen out of the different theological expressions by which this faith was expressed. They there-fore encourage the clergy and faithful of their Churches to even greater endeavours at removing the obstacles which still prevent complete commun-ion among them. This should be done with love, with openness to the promptings of the Holy Spirit, and with mutual respect for each other and each other's Church. They particularly exhort the scholars of their Churches and of all Christian communities to penetrate more deeply into the mystery of Christ with humility and fidelity to the apostolic traditions, so the fruits of their reflections may help the Church in her service to the world, which the Incarnate Son of God has redeemed.

This world, which God so loved as to send his only begotten Son, is torn by strife, by injustice and by the inhumanity of man towards man. As Christian pastors, the Pope and the Patriarch raise their common appeal to the leaders of the peoples to increase the efforts towards achieving lasting peace among nations and towards removing the obstacles which prevent so many men from enjoying the fruits of justice and religious freedom. Their appeal is directed to all areas of the world and in particular to that land hallowed by the preaching, the death, and the resurrection of our Lord and Saviour Jesus Christ.

III. The Common Declaration of Pope Paul VI and the Coptic Orthodox Patriarch, Pope Shenouda III: Rome, May 10, 1973[3]

Paul VI, Bishop of Rome and Pope of the Catholic Church, and Shenouda III, Pope of Alexandria and Patriarch of the See of St. Mark, give thanks in the Holy Spirit to God that, after the great event of the return of relics of St. Mark to Egypt, relations have further developed between the Churches of Rome and Alexandria so that they have now been able to meet personally together. At the end of their meetings and conversations they wish to state together the following:

We have met in the desire to deepen the relations between our Churches and to find concrete ways to overcome the obstacles in the way of our real cooperation in the service of our Lord Jesus Christ who has given us the ministry of reconciliation, to reconcile the world to himself (2 Cor 5:18-20).

In accordance with our apostolic traditions transmitted to our Churches and preserved therein, and in conformity with the early three ecumenical

---

[3]   English original: *Acta Apostolicae Sedis* 65 (1973) 299-301.

councils, we confess one faith in the one triune God, the divinity of the only begotten Son of God, the Second Person of the Holy Trinity, the Word of God, the effulgence of his glory, and the express image of his substance, who for us was incarnate, assuming for himself a real body with a rational soul, and who shared with us our humanity but without sin. We confess that our Lord and God and Saviour and King of us all, Jesus Christ, is perfect God with respect to his divinity, perfect man with respect to his humanity. In him, his divinity is united with his humanity in a real, perfect union without mingling, without commixtion, without confusion, without alteration, without division, without separation. His divinity did not separate from his humanity for an instant, not for the twinkling of an eye. He who is God eternal and invisible became visible in the flesh, and took upon himself the form of a servant. In him are preserved all the properties of the divinity and all the properties of the humanity, together in a real, perfect, indivisible, and inseparable union.

The divine life is given to us and is nourished in us through the seven sacraments of Christ in his Church: baptism, chrism (confirmation), holy Eucharist, penance, anointing of the sick, matrimony, and holy orders.

We venerate the Virgin Mary, Mother of the True Light, and we confess that she is ever virgin, the God-bearer. She intercedes for us, and as the Theotokos, excels in her dignity all angelic hosts.

We have, to a large degree, the same understanding of the Church, founded upon the Apostles, and of the important role of ecumenical and local councils. Our spirituality is well and profoundly expressed in our rituals and in the Liturgy of the Mass, which comprises the centre of our public prayer and the culmination of our incorporation into Christ in his Church. We keep the fasts and feasts of our faith. We venerate the relics of the saints and ask the intercession of the angels and of the saints, the living and the departed. These compose a cloud of witnesses in the Church. They and we look in hope for the second coming of our Lord when his glory will be revealed to judge the living and the dead.

We humbly recognize that our Churches are not able to give more perfect witness to this new life in Christ because of existing divisions which have behind them centuries of difficult history. In fact, since the year 451, theological differences, nourished and widened by non-theological factors, have sprung up. These differences cannot be ignored. In spite of them, however, we are rediscovering ourselves as Churches with a common inheritance and are reaching out with determination and confidence in the Lord to achieve the fullness and perfection of that unity which is his gift.

As an aid to accomplishing this task, we are setting up a joint commission representing our Churches, whose function will be to guide common study in the fields of Church tradition, patristics, liturgy, theology, history, and practical problems, so that by cooperation in common we may seek to resolve, in a spirit of mutual respect, the differences existing between our Churches and be able to proclaim together the Gospel in ways which correspond to the authentic message of the Lord and to the needs and hopes of today's world. At the same time we express our gratitude and encouragement to other groups of Catholic and Orthodox scholars and pastors who devote their efforts to common activity in these and related fields.

With sincerity and urgency we recall that true charity, rooted in total fidelity to the one Lord Jesus Christ and in mutual respect for each one's traditions, is an essential element of this search for perfect communion.

In the name of this charity, we reject all forms of proselytism, in the sense of acts by which persons seek to disturb each other's communities by recruiting new members from each other through methods, or because of attitudes of mind, which are opposed to the exigencies of Christian love or to what should characterize the relationships between Churches. Let it cease, where it may exist. Catholics and Orthodox should strive to deepen charity and cultivate mutual consultation, reflection and cooperation in the social and intellectual fields and should humble themselves before God, supplicating him who, as he has begun this work in us, will bring it to fruition.

As we rejoice in the Lord who has granted us the blessings of this meeting, our thoughts reach out to the thousands of suffering and homeless Palestinian people. We deplore any misuse of religious arguments for political purposes in this area. We earnestly desire and look for a just solution for the Middle East crisis so that true peace with justice should prevail, especially in that land which was hallowed by the preaching, death, and resurrection of our Lord and Saviour Jesus Christ, and by the life of the Blessed Virgin Mary, whom we venerate together as the Theotokos. May God, the giver of all good gifts, hear our prayers and bless our endeavours.

IV. The Common Declaration of Pope John Paul II and Syrian Orthodox Patriarch Moran Mor Ignatius Zakka I Iwas: June 23, 1984[4]

(1) His Holiness John Paul II, Bishop of Rome and Pope of the Catholic Church, and His Holiness Moran Mor Ignatius Zakka I Iwas, Patriarch of Antioch and All the East and Supreme Head of the Universal Syrian Ortho-

---

[4]   *Information Service* 55 (1984/II-III) 61-63.

dox Church, kneel down with full humility in front of the exalted and extolled heavenly throne of our Lord Jesus Christ, giving thanks for this glorious opportunity which has been granted them to meet together in his love in order to strengthen further the relationship between their two sister Churches, the Church of Rome and the Syrian Orthodox Church of Antioch—the relationship already excellent through the joint initiative of Their Holinesses of blessed memory Pope Paul VI and Patriarch Moran Mor Ignatius Jacoub III.

(2) Their Holinesses Pope John Paul II and Patriarch Zakka I wish solemnly to widen the horizon of their brotherhood and affirm herewith the terms of the deep spiritual communion which already unites them and the prelates, clergy, and faithful of both their Churches, to consolidate these ties of faith, hope, and love, and to advance in finding a wholly common ecclesial life.

(3) First of all, Their Holinesses confess the faith of their two Churches, formulated by Nicene Council of 325 and generally known as "the Nicene Creed." The confusions and schisms that occurred between their Churches in the later centuries, they realize today, in no way affect or touch the substance of their faith, since these arose only because of differences in terminology and culture and in the various formulae adopted by different theological schools to express the same matter. Accordingly, we find today no real basis for the sad division and schisms that subsequently arose between us concerning the doctrine of incarnation. In words and life we confess the true doctrine concerning Christ our Lord, notwithstanding the differences in interpretation of such a doctrine which arose at the time of the Council of Chalcedon.

(4) Hence we wish to reaffirm solemnly our profession of common faith in the incarnation of our Lord Jesus Christ, as Pope Paul VI and Patriarch Moran Mor Ignatius Jacoub III did in 1971. They denied that there was any difference in the faith they confessed in the mystery of the Word of God made flesh and become truly man. In our turn we confess that he became incarnate for us, taking to himself a real body with a rational soul. He shared our humanity in all things except sin. We confess that our Lord and our God, our Saviour and the King of all, Jesus Christ, is perfect God as to his divinity and perfect man as to his humanity. In him his divinity is united to his humanity. This union is real, perfect, without blending or mingling, without confusion, without alteration, without division, without the least separation. He who is God eternal and indivisible became visible in the flesh and took the form of servant. In him are united, in a real, perfect, indivisible and inseparable way, divinity and humanity, and in him all their properties are present and active.

(5) Having the same conception of Christ, we confess also the same conception of his mystery. Incarnate, dead and risen again, our Lord, God,

and Saviour has conquered sin and death. Through him during the time be-tween Pentecost and the Second Coming, the period which is also the last phase of time, it is given to man to experience the new creation, the kingdom of God, the transforming ferment (cf. Mt 13:33) already present in our midst. For this God has chosen a new people, his holy Church which is the body of Christ. Through the word and through the sacraments, the Holy Spirit acts in the Church to call everybody and make them members of this Body of Christ. Those who believe are baptized in the Holy Spirit in the name of the Holy Trinity to form one body, and through the holy sacrament of the anointing of confirmation their faith is perfected and strengthened by the same Spirit.

(6) Sacramental life finds in the holy Eucharist its fulfillment and its summit, in such a way that it is through the Eucharist that the Church most profoundly realizes and reveals its nature. Through the holy Eucharist, the event of Christ's Pasch expands throughout the Church. Through holy bap-tism and confirmation, indeed, the members of Christ are anointed by the Holy Spirit, grafted on to Christ; and through the holy Eucharist the Church becomes what she is destined to be through baptism and confirmation. By communion with the body and blood of Christ, the faithful grow in that mys-terious divinization which by the Holy Spirit makes them dwell in the Son as children of the Father.

(7) The other sacraments, which the Catholic Church and the Syrian Orthodox Church of Antioch hold together in one and the same succession of apostolic ministry, i.e., holy orders, matrimony, reconciliation of penitents, and anointing of the sick, are ordered to that celebration of the holy Eucha-rist which is the centre of sacramental life and the chief visible expression of ecclesial communion. This communion of Christians with each other and of local Churches united around their lawful bishops is realized in the gathered community which confesses the same faith, which reaches forward in hope of the world to come and in expectation of the Saviour's return, and is anointed by the Holy Spirit, who dwells in it with charity that never fails.

(8) Since it is the chief expression of Christian unity between the faith-ful and between bishops and priests, the holy Eucharist cannot yet be concelebrated by us. Such celebration supposes a complete identity of faith such as does not yet exist between us. Certain questions, in fact, still need to be resolved touching the Lord's will for his Church, as also the doctrinal implications and canonical details of the traditions proper to our communi-ties, which have been too long separated.

(9) Our identity in faith, though not yet complete, entitles us to en-visage collaboration between our Churches in pastoral care, in situations

which nowadays are frequent both because of the dispersion of our faithful throughout the world and because of the precarious conditions of these difficult times. It is not rare, in fact, for our faithful to find access to a priest of their own Church materially or morally impossible. Anxious to meet their needs and with their spiritual benefit in mind, we authorize them in such cases to ask for the sacraments of penance, Eucharist and anointing of the sick from lawful priests of either of our two sister Churches, when they need them. It would be a logical corollary of collaboration in pastoral care to cooperate in priestly formation and theological education. Bishops are encouraged to promote sharing of facilities for theological education where they judge it to be advisable. While doing this we do not forget that we must still do all in our power to achieve the full visible communion between the Catholic Church and the Syrian Orthodox Church of Antioch and ceaselessly implore our Lord to grant us unity which alone will enable us to give to the world a fully unanimous Gospel witness.

(10) Thanking the Lord who has allowed us to meet and enjoy the consolation of the faith we hold in common (cf. Rom 1:12) and to proclaim before the world the mystery of the person of the Word Incarnate and of his saving work, the unshakable foundation of that common faith, we pledge ourselves solemnly to do all that in us lies to remove the last obstacles still hindering full communion between the Catholic Church and the Syrian Orthodox Church of Antioch, so that with one heart and voice we may preach the word: "The true light that enlightens every man" and "that all who believe in his name may become the children of God" (cf. Jn 1:9-12).

Other Official Documents Pertaining to Oriental Orthodox–Roman Catholic Relations

I. Letter of Cardinals Johannes Willebrands and Paul Philippe to the Coptic Catholic Patriarch, Stephanos I Sidarouss: March 29, 1977[1]

Your Beatitude,

During the visit of Your Beatitude to Rome last November, we had occasion to discuss the dialogue between the Catholic Church and the Coptic Orthodox Church. We were able to recognise that certain factors could harm relations between our Churches, and we examined how these relations might be further developed. The joint committee, established following the visit of His Holiness Pope Shenouda III to the Holy Father in 1973, presented certain recommendations to the Holy See for the furtherance of the dialogue. In addition, there have been several exchanges of messages between the representatives of the Coptic Orthodox Church and those of the Catholic Church.

In these circumstances we thought it useful to share with Your Beatitude and your brothers in the episcopate the thinking of the Holy See on this subject, such as it has been expressed on various occasions in recent months, above all in a letter from the Cardinal Secretary of State[2] addressed to Patriarch Shenouda, and also in the letter of the President of the Secretariat for Promoting Christian Unity sent to His Excellency Bishop Samuel.[3]

As Your Beatitude knows, the Holy See considers the dialogue with the Coptic Orthodox Church, in the search for full communion, as one of the most important dialogues of the Catholic Church. The Coptic Orthodox Church is recognised as a Church possessing apostolic succession and a faith and sacramental life which, in the words of the Holy Father (Speech for the Week of Prayer for Christian Unity 1972) put it in an "almost complete" communion with the Catholic Church. In ecumenical dialogue the Coptic Orthodox Church is a partner with whom the Catholic Church seeks disin-

---

[1] English translation published in the Pontifical Council for Promoting Unity's *Information Service* 76 (1991/I) 23-26. This text was closely examined by the national consultation at its 1992 meeting.

[2] At that time the Secretary of State (the first position in the Vatican after the Pope) was the Frenchman Cardinal Jean Villot. He held that office from 1969 until his death in March 1979.

[3] Coptic Orthodox Bishop Samuel had been an observer at Vatican II, and directed the ecumenical relations of the Coptic Church. He was killed on October 6, 1981, during the assassination of Egyptian President Anwar Sadat.

terested collaboration in order to co-operate in the development of the Christian life of her faithful and to open the way to a more perfect communion.

The Coptic Catholic Church has a specific role to play in this dialogue which she carries out according to the principles of the conciliar Decree on Ecumenism and the statements of the Holy Father. An essential part of this dialogue is the deepening of the spiritual and apostolic life of the Church. Hence the need to partake in the pastoral renewal occurring throughout the Catholic Church following the Second Vatican Council.

It is in this context that His Eminence Cardinal Jean Villot, in the name of the Holy Father, expressed his regret to His Holiness Shenouda III, that the episcopal nomination of the Catholic patriarchal Vicar, His Excellency Monsignor Athanasios Abadir, might have been thought by the Patriarch to be an obstacle to the search for unity. The Pope, who continues to disapprove of acts of proselytism between our Christian communities is really convinced that the unity hoped for among all those who believe in Christ cannot come about without all the faithful, clergy and laity feeling in themselves the pain of division and ceaselessly meditating on the prayer of Christ "that they may all be one" (Jn 17:21). But this can only come about if Christians live deeply the whole message of the Gospel.

The preaching of this message, wrote the Cardinal Secretary of State, and the encouragement of both clergy and laity to live it out fully, constitute an essential task of the bishops. In this perspective, the nomination of a bishop, when it is required by the pastoral needs of the faithful, is truly an act by which the Church shows its desire to maintain and strengthen her faithfulness to Christ.

The Catholic Church receives with joy all the news concerning the vitality of the Coptic Orthodox Church and rejoices in it. Likewise we would hope that the nomination of a new Catholic pastor, who must see to the deepening of the faith of the Catholics, might be thought of as being able to bring with it a greater reconciliation among brothers, according to the will of Christ.

The Holy See, concluded Cardinal Villot, considers as positive the fact that the Coptic Catholic Patriarchal Synod chose as patriarchal vicar the only Coptic Catholic priest who was a member of the joint committee of the Catholic Church and the Coptic Orthodox Church. Indeed, this choice seems to show a desire to further tighten the different kinds of links which already unite Catholic Copts and Orthodox Copts. Such is the election of a pastor who, whilst helping the Coptic Catholic Patriarch to guide his flock, would also be sympathetic in heart and mind to dialogue with his Coptic Orthodox brethren.

One important feature in the development of the dialogue is the work of the joint committee drawn from our two Churches. In a meeting held in Vienna during August 1976, certain recommendations were drawn up and submitted to the Catholic authorities. Some of these recommendations were connected with the concern of the Orthodox Copts to ensure that dialogue and mutual collaboration did not create confusion among their faithful or open the way to an expansion of the Catholic Church at the expense of the Orthodox.

These recommendations have been the object of an in-depth study on the part of the Holy See. The Cardinal President of the Secretariat for Promoting Christian Unity informed Bishop Samuel of our reactions in a letter written with the full agreement of the Cardinal Prefect of the Congregation for Eastern Churches.

In this letter the need was recognised for the theological dialogue to be directed towards the re-establishment of full communion between our two Churches, without it getting lost in purely academic exercises.

The Orthodox had the impression that since their dialogue was with the Catholic Church, it was enough to have contact with the Church of Rome alone in order to reach certain decisions. But Cardinal Willebrands pointed out that although the Holy See remains the principal interlocutor, it is the local Church with its bishop which is first of all responsible for the Christian life of the community. Doubtless the Holy See can stimulate and coordinate this activity, encourage and guide it, or correct it where there are abuses, but the Church of Rome does not at all take the place of the local Church. The Church of Rome may favour certain concrete proposals; she may encourage them and assist in their realisation, both morally and materially, in active cooperation with the local Church.

The letter confirms that the Catholic Church agrees completely with the following: that none of its activities should be used to create confusion among Orthodox faithful, nor open the way to the expansion of the Catholic Church at the expense of the Coptic Orthodox. The search for full communion must take place in an atmosphere of mutual trust, reciprocal respect, and continuing consultation. This atmosphere needs to be further developed, although one remains conscious of various errors, both in the past and even in the present.

We have informed Bishop Samuel that the Catholic authorities here accept a large number of the Vienna recommendations; indeed, we think it possible for members of religious congregations to work directly at the service of the religious and pastoral needs of the Orthodox Church. They could work according to the pastoral instructions of the Orthodox authorities in a manner analogous to that in which they already follow the pastoral instructions of the Catholic authorities.

The Vienna statement recommended that Catholic institutions engaged in social and educational activities might invite members of the Orthodox Church nominated by their authorities to become members of their administrative or governing bodies, and that a study be made of the social projects already in existence in areas where all (or almost all) the Christians are Orthodox. This would be in order to discover what role might be given to the Orthodox in their direction and in their day-to-day activity. The Catholic authorities encourage the application of such recommendations, whilst taking account of the statutes of these organisations and their financial autonomy.

We encourage international Catholic financial aid agencies to support Orthodox projects in the same way in which they support Catholic projects. Furthermore, on the occasion of the sale or transfer of properties belonging to Catholic institutions, we suggest that preference be given to the Orthodox. However, the statutes of the organisations which own the works, as well as the wishes of their founders or benefactors, must be taken into account.

In the same letter, the President of the Secretariat for Promoting Christian Unity let it be known that the recommendation that the Catholic Church should not set up new parishes, dioceses, or institutions such as monasteries or convents for a period of five years, was unacceptable in the form in which it had been drawn up. No such absolute prohibition could be imposed upon the bishops who are responsible for their own faithful and who must use whatever means they consider necessary to fulfill this responsibility.

However, we recognise that the setting up of Catholic institutions has at times resulted in the expansion of the Catholic Church at the expense of the Orthodox. Therefore we could accept a formulation of a recommendation which states that the Catholic Church carry out its pastoral activities within the framework of structures and institutions already existing, and that any changes be determined uniquely by the needs of its own faithful.

The Coptic Orthodox have been assured that the Catholic Church does not consider them as objects of a "mission" and that it is important that all pastoral work among Orthodox be undertaken with the knowledge, agreement and cooperation of the Orthodox authorities, and without the intention of having people pass from one Church to the other. For this reason it is necessary that there be frequent and regular contacts between Catholic bishops and religious superiors and those of the Orthodox Church. These contacts are deemed necessary in order to create that atmosphere of mutual respect

115

and trust which is lacking at present, to meet the pastoral needs of the Christians, and to sort out particular items which could be a source of misunderstanding or friction.

Once again the Holy See commends the work of the local joint committee. Moreover, it is convinced that it is mainly by means of regular systematic consultations between the authorities of the two Churches, that the fears, worries and desires expressed in the Vienna Report can be dealt with.

In his letter to Bishop Samuel, Cardinal Willebrands spoke clearly and frankly about the practice of some Orthodox of "rebaptising" Catholics who pass to the Orthodox Church. By this custom, the Orthodox Church puts in doubt the very existence of the Catholic Church with its sacraments, its liturgy, and its hierarchy. Many Catholics find in this behaviour an obstacle to their participation in the ecumenical movement. Therefore, we ask that this practice be ended, though we are not demanding any public statement on this matter.

In another letter, the Secretariat for Promoting Christian Unity also informed Bishop Samuel of our thinking in the question of the passage of Christians from one Church to another. We recognise the possibility of such cases occurring for reasons of faith and out of a deep personal conviction, of which the local bishop is the judge. Nevertheless, when it is a matter of groups of persons able to form a community, the bishop will make a very close investigation of their motives. If these initiatives are due to a desire to withdraw, for no matter what reason, from the authority of their own bishop or parish priest, that is not sufficient motive. Such a request to pass to the Catholic Church should be refused, and the Orthodox authorities must be informed of such proposals. In collaboration with the Orthodox authorities, a solution must be sought in such a way as to restore peace to the community.

Your Beatitude can see the importance which we give to developing relations between Catholic and Orthodox bishops, whether on an individual basis or on the level of the hierarchies as such. It is important in the search for full communion that the Catholic and the Orthodox authorities really acknowledge one another as brothers in the episcopate, with pastoral concerns which transcend the present divisions and necessitate brotherly collaboration.

Recently, during the visit of the four Catholic members of the local joint committee, of which Bishop Kabès is co-president, we had an opportunity for friendly discussions which helped us better appreciate both the difficulties being encountered in this important stage of dialogue with the Coptic Orthodox Church, and the common desire to overcome them.

We had occasion to clearly underline, once again, the thinking and hopes of the Holy See. It has been agreed that we must together overcome the lack of trust which separates the Coptic Catholics from the Coptic Orthodox. Hence the need for regular contacts between the two hierarchies to prevent misunderstandings, to deepen mutual respect and to favour the pastoral care of all Christians. Similarly, whilst respecting the autonomy of Catholic pastors to take the decisions they judge necessary for the pastoral care of their own people, these meetings and exchanges are especially recommended when it is a matter of taking important pastoral and organisational decisions.

During the meetings in Rome, the hope was expressed that the Assembly of Ordinaries might become an appropriate means for the encouragement of interritual collaboration in the work for ecumenism as well.

As regards the collaboration offered by religious and other individuals and institutions to the Coptic Orthodox pastors, it has been decided that this collaboration would follow the general orientations of the Catholic Church, in conformity with their constitutions or statutes and according to the instructions of the hierarchy.

To conclude, the Holy See commends the local joint committee to the Catholic hierarchy. The committee's work is of particular importance for ecumenical activity in Egypt. The Sacred Congregation for the Eastern Churches and this Secretariat are very grateful to their colleagues for their work in this area.

In writing to Your Beatitude, we wished to offer these reflections in the hope that they might help the Catholic Church in Egypt fulfill its essential role in the search for unity between Catholics and Orthodox, a search which will lead the two sister Churches to re-establish the full communion which is Christ's will. The Holy Father has already told Your Beatitude that he is sure that the Catholics in Egypt will collaborate fully in this task. We entrust this task to your pastoral care and that of the members of your Holy Synod, and all the Catholic Ordinaries of Egypt, of whose assembly Your Beatitude is president.

With every fraternal good wish,

Yours Sincerely in Christ,

Johannes Cardinal Willebrands, President
Secretariat for Promoting Christian Unity

Paul Cardinal Philippe, Prefect
Sacred Congregation for Eastern Churches

II. Principles for Guiding the Search for Unity Between the Catholic Church and the Coptic Orthodox Church[4]

Preamble

Through meetings of an official mixed commission established in 1973, through unofficial theological consultations starting in 1971 and through other exchanges, official and informal, the Catholic Church and the Coptic Orthodox Church have made important progress in understanding the deep bonds of faith and Christian life which exist between them, despite a separation which has lasted fifteen centuries. We have overcome the difficulties of the past concerning our faith in the mystery of the Word Incarnate and we can now profess in common our faith in the mystery of our redemption. We possess the same priesthood received from the Apostles and thus celebrate the same Eucharist of the Lord whose members we become through the same baptism. We share many other aspects of the Christian life proclaimed by the Apostles and handed on by the Fathers of the Church.

At the same time, there are some dogmatic and canonical divergences which prevent us from enjoying that full communion which at one time existed between the Churches of Rome and Alexandria. Serious efforts have been made to overcome these divergences. However, it seemed useful to review these efforts, to register their positive aspects and discern the deficiencies up to now.

The election of His Holiness Pope John Paul II seemed an appropriate occasion for this review. His Holiness Pope Shenouda III has sent an official delegation of the Coptic Orthodox Church to bring his greetings to the new Bishop of Rome, to express his concern about the dialogue in course and to discuss with responsible officials in Rome ways by which this dialogue may be improved and strengthened towards achieving its goal of full communion between the two Churches.

The participants in these conversations were greatly encouraged by the message of Pope Shenouda III and the warm response of Pope John Paul II. The texts of these messages contain very important reflections and guidelines for continuing the common search. In addition, the participants recognized that many important elements are to be found in the various reports and communications made over the past eight years. However, if these ele-

---

[4] These principles, with the attached protocol, were prepared on June 23, 1979 by the members of the joint international commission between the Catholic Church and the Coptic Orthodox Church. They were then submitted to Pope John Paul II and to Pope Shenouda III, who approved and signed both documents. Text in *Information Service* 76 (1991/I) 30-32.

ments are to bear fruit among the clergy and faithful of both Churches, they must be understood within the context of certain general principles which can guide the search for unity in a spirit of mutual trust and confidence and of renewed dedication to the command of the Lord of the Church "that all may be one."

These principles are now presented to our Churches with the hope that they will be seriously studied and assimilated by our people, and with the prayer that the Holy Spirit may guide us in applying them effectively to the work which still lies ahead.

(1) The objective of our efforts is a full communion of faith expressing itself in communion in sacramental life and in the harmony of mutual relations between our two sister Churches in the one People of God.

(2) We are two Apostolic Churches in which, by virtue of the Apostolic succession we possess the full sacramental life, particularly the Eucharist, even if Eucharistic communion has not yet been achieved between us in so far as we have not completely resolved the divergences among us.

(3) The resolution of these divergences is all the more important, therefore, in order that our Churches may give more adequate expression to the communion which already exists in an imperfect way among them. Thus they will be able to give more perfect witness to their faith and their life in Christ than they can in their present state of division, since local Catholic Churches everywhere and the Coptic Church will then fully recognize each other as the realization in their places of the one, holy, catholic and apostolic Church.

(4) The unity we envisage in no way means absorption of one by the other or domination by one over the other. It is at the service of each to help each live better the proper gifts it has received from God's Spirit.

(5) The unity presupposes that our Churches continue to have the right and power to govern themselves according to their own traditions and disciplines.

(6) This legitimate autonomy does not deny the necessity of mutual relations between our Churches. When the Churches live more closely together in communion of faith and mutual charity, they will develop new contacts and patterns of relations which will indicate how to deal with questions of common interest and concern. This process will also help the Churches to arrive to a better understanding of the meaning and extent of primacy in the Church, a concept which exists in both our Churches but about which there remain canonical and doctrinal differences preventing our full communion. In the meantime, important questions of faith, of pastoral problems, of mutual need can be treated by brotherly communications and consultations between the primates or by other means which will be judged useful.

(7) It is in the light of all the foregoing principles that we will seek to resolve the differences which still exist among us concerning our understanding of the structures through which the unity and the integrity of the faith of the Church are to be served.

(8) It is in the perspective of the search for this unity that we understand that the pastoral activity, mutual collaboration and common witness should take place at present in Egypt. None of these can have as their objective the passing of people from one Church to another. They are to serve the entire Christian community in Egypt. It is particularly important therefore that there be frequent and regular contacts between Catholic bishops and religious superiors and those of the Orthodox Church: (a) to create an atmosphere of trust and mutual confidence; (b) to meet the serious pastoral needs of the faithful of both communities; (c) to avoid misunderstandings which may arise; (d) to resolve specific cases which could be a source of misunderstanding or friction. Frequent contacts at all levels of Church life will also help avoid words, articles, homilies, instructions and attitudes which might wound each other's Churches, in their leaders or in their faithful.

(9) All this should be guided by and be in conformity with the principles stated in various communications made by the See of Rome to the Catholic Bishops of Egypt and to His Holiness Pope Shenouda III.

(10) Even if we do not adopt all the positions of the other, we should respect those positions as part of the historical heritage of the other and not exclude the possibility of reaching agreement about them.

(11) Once unity is achieved, the richness of the various Christian traditions existing in Egypt would find clear and legitimate expression for the enrichment of all within the one Coptic Church under the leadership of the Pope of Alexandria and Patriarch of the See of St. Mark.

(12) We recognize that unity is God's gift to his Church. Its concrete expression should be in accordance with the living tradition of each Church which allows for new insights and a deeper understanding of how God wishes the Churches to meet the problems presenting themselves to all Christians today and to serve the world in unity and love.

Protocol

(1) We request official reaction to the principles by the authorities of both Churches as soon as possible, and not later than the end of October. If modifications have been made, a small committee will meet immediately to discuss them and reach a common agreement about them.

(2) The approved document will be communicated by each Church to its bishops and published for the use of other persons and groups affected by it.

(3) We feel that the composition and the functions of the Joint Mixed Commission and the Local Joint Committee need further review and reform.

(4) In the meantime, two committees will be formed: one for directing studies and one for guiding practical implications. So that they can meet easily and frequently and be able to adhere to a regular timetable of work, these committees should be small, composed of two or three members from each Church.

(5) Both committees should use freely the services of other experts and not feel that the permanent members must do the bulk of the work.

(6) The committee for practical implications will set up at least three subcommittees: for schools, for social institutions, for pastoral projects. Each of these will have the responsibility to study the possibilities of cooperation in their particular area. They will seek to enlist the support and concrete activity of persons and institutions who can engage in this cooperation. There should be regular and frequent reporting on their work, with a minimum of three times a year.

(7) The committees—with their subcommittees—advise concerned persons about the principles which have been developed at the Rome conversations of June 1979, about the possibilities for concrete action, etc. They will help coordinate this action. Where questions may arise about the application or the non-application of the principles accepted, the matter should be brought to the immediate competent authority or, if this procedure is not effective, to the higher authorities, as the case may require.

(8) One of the first priorities of the two committees will be to establish a programme and priorities. Basing themselves on the four commission reports (but not restricted to them), the committees will provide for a detailed outline of the theoretical and practical studies necessary for assisting the move towards unity, and determine the priorities and relations among these as well as the people from in and outside Egypt most indicated to take part in them.

(9) What is of particular importance is that a programme be planned and implemented as soon as possible for bringing to the attention of the clergy and laity of both Churches the principles which have been determined and the progressive action which can be taken to implement them. No serious search for unity between our Churches can be carried forward without an informed and sympathetic participation of the whole Church. It is recommended that the various proposals presented by the Joint Commission and the Local Joint Com-

mittee for achieving this and for ensuring cooperation among the hierarchies of our Churches be reexamined and implemented.

III. The Joint Communiqué Published at the End of the Visit of Armenian Catholicos Karekin II Sarkissian to Pope John Paul II: Rome, April 15-19, 1983[5]

(1) The meeting between the Catholicos of Cilicia and the Bishop of Rome, in the Paschal light of the Holy Year of the Redemption 1983, opens a new stage in the relations between our Churches. For over twenty years, fraternal dialogue had progressed in a spirit of charity and of truth and in a number of different ways: the fruitful participation of the observers of the Catholicossate in the labours of Vatican Council II; the meeting of Pope Paul VI and the Catholicos Khoren I of blessed memory; common research in theology; local instances of pastoral collaboration; positive contributions to Christian unity and to social justice within the framework of various requirements of the ecumenical movement on the international, regional, and local levels. But today our Churches are called upon to respond together to more and more urgent appeals, and this meeting in the name of their common Lord confirms them in their common desire to respond to these.

(2) There is first of all the urgency of the full communion of our Churches in view of their essential mission: the salvation of mankind today. On this third Sunday of Easter when the Armenian Church is celebrating "the Church of the Universe" (*Ashkharhamadour*) the meeting between the pastors of our Churches witnesses to the importance of direct and personal relations between brothers, servants of the sole Saviour of men; and these will be continued into the future. Moreover, it is important that there be continued common theological research—the dialogue of faith—animated by the more and more clear and refined awareness that, within the unity of the faith diversity is a divine richness and an indispensable condition of the unity of the ecclesial communion.

Our Churches also have before them an immense field of cooperation where they can henceforth advance and work out, in mutual understanding, esteem, trust, and an effective charity: the theological formation of both clerics and lay people, collaboration in the catechetical instruction of the young and of adults, the practical solution of situations of common pastoral concern, social action, cultural promotion, humanitarian services. . . . In all these

---

[5]   Published by the Secretariat for Promoting Christian Unity (Rome) and the Secretariat of the Catholicosate of the Great House of Cilicia (Antelias, Lebanon). English version in the Secretariat for Promoting Christian Unity's *Information Service* 51 (1983/I-II) 40-41.

domains where the Spirit of the Lord is urging us to witness to Christ, Son of God our Saviour, it is certain that without neglecting the structures of collaboration on the international and regional levels, priority is to be given on the level of the local Churches. Just as indeed the risen Christ is "manifested in our midst" in the celebration of the divine Liturgy (cf. the kiss of peace in the Eucharist according to the Armenian tradition), so also is he manifested in the midst of all by the divine Diaconia of his Church as servant of men.

(3) If in the world of today all the Churches have become "frontier" Churches in existential relation with other religious or ideological world-views, this is especially true in the case of the local Churches of the Middle East. Such has been the particular vocation of the Armenian Church since the very beginnings, and it is therein engaged in our days within the framework of Christian witness in that region and in the other countries of its diaspora.

But the road along which the search for unity has already made our Churches advance opens out, in the present decade, on another matter of urgency for the well-being of all men: the rights of man, or better, the divine dignity of man, of each individual man. We must labour here together, not only with all men of good will but also in the clarity of our faith and the certitude of our Christian hope. This implies our common service of the dignity of persons as well as of the right of peoples to their legitimate national aspirations and to the cultural identity of their origin. But, in order that humanity today may be able to acknowledge and promote the divine dignity of man and justice for the peoples, our Churches can follow but one road: not that of the "powers of this world" (1 Cor 2), but the one who is the Way of Life through the Truth (Jn 14:6). Thus, through all their trials, our Churches exist in this world only to serve, revealing thereby their Lord, the unique Servant and Saviour of all. In this month of April in particular, during which the Armenian people recall their martyrs, those living witnesses of the Christian faith and of the basic human rights, our Churches unite with all the Churches and all the peoples who are engaged in the service of the same sacred ideals.

(4) Our Churches wish to respond by an active witness, in collaboration with the other Churches, to this appeal, this cry for more justice, which rises from the depths of humanity at this end of the second millennium. This witness is urgent, particularly in the region of the Middle East, where it will involve both developing understanding, respect, and cooperation between men regardless of their religious affiliation, and working to assure all peoples of the region harmonious development of their identity, of their liberty, and of their culture in peace and justice.

In particular as regards Lebanon where there is taking place the decisive struggle of hope versus despair in view of its unity, of its integrity and of its sovereignty, our Churches are engaged in reinforcing the eternal bonds that unite Christians not only among themselves but also with their brothers of the other communities of their common fatherland: what is involved here is the fundamental values of their country and those of the other countries of the world.

The Easter meeting of the "Sunday of the Church of the Universe" where our two Churches have shared at the source of prayer, of light and of love, participates in the unending Day of the Resurrection of their Lord: it opens toward new beginnings. "Christ is risen from the tomb! Blessed be the resurrection of Christ!" (*Chriados hariav i meremotz! orhnial e haroutioun'n Chrisdossi!*)

IV. Speech of Pope John Paul II to Ethiopian Orthodox Patriarch Paulos: Rome, June 11, 1993[6]

Your Holiness,

(1) It is truly a great joy for me to receive you and those who accompany you here today. In welcoming you, the Patriarch of the Ethiopian Orthodox Church, it is a beloved brother that I greet, one who represents a Church to which I feel very close.

In this time of Pentecost when we celebrate the outpouring of the Holy Spirit, who has gathered into one those who were once scattered, I extend most willingly, dear brother, the hand of welcome.

Your presence in Rome reminds us of that long tradition of Ethiopian pilgrims, who since the Middle Ages have come to Rome in great numbers to venerate the tomb of the Prince of the Apostles. To them my predecessors always accorded cordial hospitality within the Vatican itself. I therefore see your visit as a carrying forward of that venerable tradition, but above all as the visible expression of the profound communion that we have been rediscovering together for some years. How marvelous are the works of the spirit of God! For we, who had almost thought of ourselves as strangers to one another, now find that we are ever more closely united by the Spirit, who is our reconciliation and the bond of peace (cf. Eph 4:3).

(2) The deep communion that exists between us, despite the vicissitudes of history, is rooted in the fundamental realities of our Christian faith. For we share the faith handed down from the Apostles, as also the same

---

6   Text in the weekly English edition of *L'Osservatore Romano*, June 16, 1993, 5, and *Information Service* 84 (1993/III-IV) 150-152.

sacraments and the same ministry, rooted in the apostolic succession. This was strongly stated in the teaching of the Second Vatican Council (cf. *Unitatis Redintegratio*, n. 15).

Today, moreover, we can affirm that we have the one faith in Christ, even though for a long time this was a source of division between us. Although our traditions used different formulations to express the same ineffable mystery of the union of humanity and divinity in the Word made Flesh, our two Churches in full accord with the apostolic faith confess both the distinction and the complete union of humanity and divinity in the person of Jesus Christ, Son of God. So it is that the Ethiopian Orthodox Church and the Catholic Church confess the same faith in him who forever remains "the Way, and the Truth, and the Life" (Jn 14:6), the Lord and Saviour of the world.

All this should spur us on to seek new and suitable ways of fostering the rediscovery of our communion in the concrete daily life of the faithful of our two Churches.

We must do all we can to heal the memories of misunderstanding in the past and to promote new attitudes based on forgiveness, mutual esteem, and respect. We must resist all hostility and every spirit of rivalry between us, so that we may engage resolutely, through mutual collaboration, in the building up of our Churches.

(3) As we guide our faithful towards the rediscovery of full communion, let us seek to avoid anything that might sow confusion in their ranks. I can assure you that such is the wish of the Catholic Bishops in Ethiopia. Catholics and Orthodox—in their recognition and respect for one another as Pastors of that part of the flock which is entrusted to each—can have no other aim than the growth and the unity of the People of God.

That is the expectation of our faithful who are convinced that "brothers who once shared the same sufferings and trials ought not to oppose one another today, but should look together at the future opening before them with promising signs of hope" (*Letter on Relations between Catholics and Orthodox*, 31 May 1991).

The field for cooperation is vast. It should begin with an improvement in fraternal relationships on all levels, but most particularly among those who have the task of leadership.

Having restored this dialogue of charity between us, we may be more confident when we ask the Lord with one heart for the gift of unity, especially on the occasion of the universal Week of Prayer for Christian Unity, for which, as you know, the theme is jointly prepared each year by the Pontifical Council for Promoting Christian Unity and the World Council of Churches, to which since its inception your Church has belonged.

Finally, the circumstances of the present time require us to work together in the pastoral domain, so as not to put any obstacle in the way of "that most holy cause, the preaching of the Gospel to all creatures" (*Unitatis Redintegratio*, n. 1).

I am thinking particularly of the formation of future priests and parish workers in which the Catholic Committee for Cultural Collaboration is already engaged by providing scholarships for Ethiopian Orthodox students so that they can pursue their studies and undertake specializations; I am thinking also of the liturgy, our ancient heritage, which, if it is to remain alive, must be accessible to the people of our day; I mention also—and it is among the most urgent of problems—pastoral work among Ethiopians who have migrated to Europe and North America: likewise, the evangelization of the young, charitable work among refugees, and all the many forms of development that are necessary in order to reconstruct the country after so many difficult years.

(4) On this auspicious occasion, I wish to reiterate to Your Holiness the deep respect in which the Ethiopian Orthodox Church is held by the Catholic Church for having maintained and preserved over the centuries the patrimony of Christian faith and culture. The baptism of the Ethiopian which is reported in the Acts of the Apostles (8:27-39) bears witness to the ancient origins of your Christian faith. Following his lead, and with the same joy, the Ethiopian people embraced the Gospel and have remained faithful to it despite the many sufferings they have had to endure, even in the recent past. The close link between faith and Ethiopian culture, the persistence of the ancient monastic tradition, the riches and splendours of your liturgy—these are among the many things which the Catholic Church observes with sincere admiration.

My dear brothers, for some days now you have been going to the principal places of pilgrimage in Rome. You have already prayed at the tomb of the Apostle Peter and you will continue this afternoon and tomorrow to visit the great Basilicas and precious Christian treasures of this venerable city. I am also happy that you are also taking the opportunity to visit living communities, both monasteries and parishes, where Christians seek to celebrate and put their faith into practice. It is my earnest prayer that these spiritual meetings between our Churches may demonstrate in a public way the strength of our desire for full communion. Through the intercession of Mary, the great Mother of God, may the Holy Spirit hasten the day when we may once more eat and drink at the same Table of the Lord.

V. Agreement Between the Catholic Church and the Malankara Syrian Orthodox Church on Interchurch Marriages[7]

This agreement between the Catholic Church and the Malankara Syrian Orthodox Church on interchurch marriages has been prepared taking into account the following elements of the *Common Declaration* of Pope John Paul II and Syrian Orthodox Patriarch Zakka I Iwas of Antioch, dated 23 June 1984:

(1) The common profession of faith between the Pope and the Patriarch on the mystery of the Incarnate Word;

(2) The common affirmation of their faith in the mystery of the Church and the sacraments;

(3) The possibility given by the declaration for a pastoral collaboration, including the mutual admission of the faithful belonging to both Churches to the reception of the sacraments of penance, Eucharist and anointing of the sick for a grave spiritual need.

Having considered the above mentioned events and declaration, the Malankara Syrian Orthodox Church and the Catholic Church agreed on the following considerations and norms.

As our two Churches believe in and confess the mystery of the Church and its sacramental reality, we consider it our duty to specify the areas of agreement in cases of marriages between the members of our two Churches.

Man and woman created in the image of God (Gen 1:26-27) are called to become sharers of the eternal divine communion. The sacrament of marriage is an image of this divine communion. Marital intimacy and self-effacing sharing are reflections of the deepest interpersonal sharing within the Trinitarian communion. Hence this intimate marital communion is divinely confirmed by Christ with the seal of unity and of indissolubility, and ordered toward the good of the spouses and the generation and education of the offspring.

> "He answered, 'Have you not read that he who made them from the beginning *made them male and female,* and said, For this reason *a man shall leave his father and mother and be joined to his wife and the two shall become one flesh?'* What therefore God has joined together, let no man put asunder" (Mt 19:46).

---

[7] This agreement, along with the attached *Pastoral Guidelines,* was drafted in November 1993 by the Commission for Dialogue between the Catholic Church and the Malankara Syrian Orthodox Church. It was released on January 25, 1994, after it was approved by the competent authorities of both Churches. Text in *Eastern Churches Journal* 1/2 (1994) 181-186, and *Information Service* 85 (1993/III-IV) 159-161.

Marriage is a great sacrament of divine communion, and St. Paul compares the mutual relationship of the husband and wife to the mystery of communion between Jesus Christ and his Church (cf. Eph 5:21-26; Tit 2:3f; 1 Pet 3:1f; Rev 18:7; 21:2). St. Paul calls it a great mystery: "This mystery is a profound one, and I am saying that it refers to Christ and the Church" (Eph 5:32). Hence we believe that the sacrament of marriage bearing the image of the eternal divine communion is also an image of the most intimate communion between the risen bridegroom with his bride, the Church.

The Church is the primordial sacrament of the eternal divine communion and, through the celebration of her sacramental mysteries, she deepens her communion with the divine spouse and enables her members to participate in the divine life.

Our two Churches accept the sacredness and indissolubility of the sacramental bond of marriage and consider the conjugal relationship as an expression of the above communion and a means to achieve self-effacing mutual love and freedom from selfishness, which was the cause of the fall of humanity.

In this theological perspective, taking into account the question of the marriages between the members of our two Churches, we consider it a matter of our pastoral concern to provide the following directives.

Our two Churches desire to foster marriages within the same ecclesial communion and consider this the norm. However, we have to accept the pastoral reality that interchurch marriages do take place. When such occasions arise, both Churches should facilitate the celebration of the sacrament of matrimony in either Church, allowing the bride/bridegroom the right and freedom to retain her/his own ecclesial communion, by providing necessary information and documents. On the occasion of these celebrations, the couple as well as their family members belonging to these two Churches are allowed to participate in the holy Eucharist in the Church where the sacrament of matrimony is celebrated. We consider it also the great responsibility of the parents to pay special attention to impart to the extent possible and in mutual accord proper ecclesial formation to their children in full harmony with the tradition of the ecclesial communion to which they have to belong.

Participants:

Roman Catholic Church
> His Excellency Bishop Pierre Duprey, Pontifical Council for
> Promoting Christian Unity, Vatican City (Co-Chairman)

His Excellency Mar Joseph Powathil, Archbishop of
Changanacherry, India
His Excellency Mar Kuriakose Kunnacherry, Bishop of
Kottayam, India
His Excellency Patrick D'Souza, Bishop of Varanasi, India
His Excellency Cyril Mar Baselios Malancharuvil,
Malankara Catholic Bishop of Battery, India
Rev. Dr. Clarence Gallagher, SJ, Rome, Italy
Rev. Dr. Matthew Vellanickal, Kottayam, India
Rev. Dr. Xavier Koodapuzha, Kottayam, India
Rev. Dr. Geevarghese Chediath, Trivandrum, India
Rev. Bernard Dubasque, Vatican City (Co-Secretary)

Malankara Syrian Orthodox Church
His Grace Dr. Thomas Mor Athanasius (Co-Chairman)
His Grace Thomas Mor Thimotheos
His Grace Yuhanon Mor Meletius
Very Rev. Prof. Joseph Cor-Episcopa Pulickaparampil
Rev. Cherian Poothicote
Rev. Dr. Adai Jacob
Rev. Kuriakose Moolayil (Co-Secretary)
Rev. R. V. Markose
Dr. D. Babu Paul
Rev. Deacon Shibu Cherian
Rev. Deacon Biji C. Markose
Rev. Deacon Saji K. V.

Pastoral Guidelines on Marriages Between Members of the Catholic Church and of the Malankara Syrian Orthodox Church[8]

(1) These guidelines are framed on the basis of the common declaration of His Holiness Pope John Paul II and His Holiness Patriarch Ignatius Zakka I Iwas.

(2) Commissions were appointed by both Churches to explore ways and means to foster the existing common affirmation of the faith and sacramental unity between the Churches.

(3) Having considered the above mentioned declaration and the unity that exists between the two Churches in faith and sacraments, both Churches

---

[8]   Applies to the Catholic Church.

have agreed to accept the reality of interchurch marriages taking place between their members.

(4) The two Churches desire to foster marriages within the same ecclesial communion and consider this as the norm. However, accepting the reality that interchurch marriages do take place at times, the two Churches have decided to facilitate the celebration of the sacrament of matrimony in either Church, allowing the bride/bridegroom the right and freedom to retain her/his own ecclesial communion, by providing necessary information and documents.

Preparation for Interchurch Marriages

(5) When the parties apply for an interchurch marriage they should be told that the marriage within the same faith is better for the harmony of the family and the upbringing of the children.

(6) If they insist on conducting the interchurch marriage they should be instructed properly about the Agreement reached between the Syrian Orthodox Church and the Catholic Church on interchurch marriages.

(7) It should be stressed that, while each partner holds his/her ecclesial faith as supreme or paramount, he/she should respect the ecclesial faith of his/her partner.

(8) A pre-marriage preparatory course and a premarital counseling session are highly recommended.

(9) The bride/bridegroom shall produce her/his baptism certificate.

(10) The priest must ensure that the bride/bridegroom is eligible for marriage.

(11) The priest should ensure that the bride/bridegroom has paid the church donations in connection with marriages according to the practice of the Churches.

(12) The bride and bridegroom, after mutual consultation, may select the church in which the marriage is to be celebrated.

(13) Written permission for interchurch marriage from the respective bishops should be obtained by the bride/bridegroom.

(14) Banns should be published in the respective Churches, which also announce that it is an interchurch marriage.

(15) Once the permission is obtained from the bishops, the respective parish priests are expected to issue the necessary documents for the conduct of marriage.

(16) Marriage in the Lent or Advent seasons is only to be conducted with the permission of the bishops.

Celebration of Interchurch Marriages

(17) The liturgical minister should be the parish priest of the church where the marriage is celebrated, or his delegate from the same ecclesial communion.

(18) There is to be no joint celebration of marriage by the ministers of both Churches. The marriage is to be blessed either by the Catholic or by the Syrian Orthodox minister. However, there could be some kind of participation at the liturgical service by the other minister who could read a scriptural passage or give a sermon.

(19) On the occasion of these celebrations, the couple and any members of their families who belong to these Churches are allowed to participate in the holy Eucharist in the church where the sacrament of matrimony is being celebrated.

(20) Proper entries must be made in the church registers, and marriage certificates should be issued for a record to be made in the register of the other church.

Pastoral Care of Catholic-Syrian Orthodox Interchurch Families

(21) The Catholic partner is to be reminded that he or she has to commit him/herself to imparting to their children proper Catholic formation, to the extent possible and in agreement with his/her partner (cf. *Directory for the Application of Principles and Norms on Ecumenism*, no. 150-151). Such formation should be fully in harmony with the Catholic tradition to which he/she belongs .

(22) The pastors of both partners are bound in conscience to provide continued pastoral care to the interchurch families in such a way as to contribute to their sanctity, unity and harmony.

(23) Each partner is to be advised to attend the liturgical celebrations of his/her respective Church, but the couple may be allowed to participate jointly in the eucharistic celebration on special occasions when this joint participation is socially required.

(24) Any declaration of the nullity of such marriages is only to be considered with the consent of the bishops concerned from both Churches.

(25) The funeral service should as far as possible be conducted according to the rite of the dead person's Church, even though he/she may be buried in either of the cemeteries, especially if the other partner is already buried there in a family tomb. ⌒

APPENDIX C

The Oriental Orthodox Churches: A Brief Description

THE ARMENIAN ORTHODOX CHURCH[1]

by Reverend Arten Ashjian

The Name of the Church

The Armenian Church, or The Church of Armenia, is also called "Apostolic" and "Orthodox," the latter being the commonly used epithet in Moslem countries.

Historical Origins

The Church of Armenia traces its origins to Thaddeus and Bartholomew, two of the twelve apostles, who are referred to as the "first enlighteners of Armenia" to distinguish them from the second enlightener, St. Gregory (d. 325). According to tradition, the two apostles were put to death in Armenia, St. Thaddeus in the year 66 and St. Bartholomew in 68.

Because of this apostolic evangelization, Christianity took root in Armenia in the period before Armenians could record their history in their own language, since the Armenian alphabet had not yet been devised. History records religious persecutions by at least three kings of Armenia during the years 100, 238, and 280. A victim of the persecution that began in the year 280 was St. Gregory, called the "enlightener" or "illuminator" of Armenia. Gregory, of the noble Parthev or Pahlavooni family, had been educated at Caesarea in Cappadocia. He entered the service of King Tiridates of Armenia, who inflicted much persecution and suffering upon him. But Gregory succeeded in converting Tiridates, who in turn helped St. Gregory convert the whole country to Christianity. Ordained a bishop in Caesarea soon after the conversion of King Tiridates, Gregory built, with the support of the King, the first Christian cathedral at Vagharshapat in 303, near Mount Ararat, then the capital of Armenia. He was directed to do this by our Lord in a vision. In memory of this, the cathedral is known as Holy Etchmiadzin, that

---

[1]   The descriptions of these Churches are based on those found in Robert F. Taft, SJ, editor, *The Oriental Orthodox Churches in the United States* (Washington, D.C.: National Conference of Catholic Bishops, 1986).

is, the place where the "Only Begotten Descended." Holy Etchmiadzin is still the official seat of the supreme head of the Armenian Orthodox Church.

Major Turning Points in History

In 325, the Armenian Church participated in the First Ecumenical Council at Nicea, with St. Aristakes, the younger son of St. Gregory the Enlightener, representing his ailing father.

The thirty-six characters of the Armenian alphabet were devised by the monk St. Mesrop in 406. The translation of the Bible was accomplished within thirty years, and the preparation of the liturgical books and translations of patristic works were undertaken by pupils of St. Mesrop and St. Sahak (Catholicos, 387-436).

In defense of the Christian faith, Armenia waged war in 451 against militarily superior Zoroastrian Persia. Outnumbered, Armenian troops under the command of St. Vartan Mamigonian lost the battle, but the war dragged on until 485, when Persia ended its campaign to force Armenians back to Zoroastrianism.

In 506 a synod of Armenian, Georgian, and Caspio-Albanian bishops assembled at Dvin, which had been the seat of the Armenian Catholicos since 485. It proclaimed the profession of faith of the Third Ecumenical Council of Ephesus (431) and rejected Nestorianism and the acts of the Council of Chalcedon (451).

The seat of the Armenian Catholicos remained at Dvin, the original residence of the Bagratid kings, until 927 when the city was sacked by invading Arabs. First the island of Aghtamar in Lake Van, and then the fortified city of Ani, became the seat of the Catholicoi for over a century, until Ani capitulated to the attacking Greeks in 1045. With the ensuing migrations of large numbers of Armenians westward, the seat of the Catholicos was established in the castle of Romkla on the Euphrates River until 1293. During the Cilician Armenian Kingdom, the Catholicate was transferred to the capital Sis. It remained there until the return of the seat to Holy Etchmiadzin in 1441.

Attempts at reunion, first with the Greek Church, then with the Latin Church, were initiated by Catholicos St. Nersess the Gracious in the twelfth century. He proposed a meeting of Armenian bishops and archimandrites to consider reunion with the Byzantine Church, but before responses could reach him, St. Nersess died in 1173 at the age of seventy-one.

In the seventh century, during the Arab occupation of the Holy City, an Armenian Patriarchate was recognized. The first Armenian Patriarch of Jerusalem, Bishop Abraham, held office from 638 to 669.

The Armenian Patriarchate of Turkey was created by the Ottoman rulers in 1461, soon after the conquest of Constantinople. In the nineteenth century, lay leaders in the Armenian community of the capital (some of them educated in France) succeeded in drawing up an Armenian statute for the general administration of the Patriarchate. The Ottoman government gave its reluctant sanction to the proposed procedure in 1863. The statute was annulled by the Turkish secular government in the 1920s.

Following the liberation of Yerevan and Etchmiadzin from Persian rule by the Russians in 1828, the Czarist government enacted in 1836 a regulation (*Polozhenie*) that formalized relations with the Catholicate of Holy Etchmiadzin.

The deportations and genocide carried out by the Turkish government against the Christian population in the provinces during World War I dealt a severe blow to the Armenian Church. Of the 5,000 clergymen living in 1915, only 400 had survived by 1923.

With the sovietization of the tiny Armenian republic where Holy Etchmiadzin was located, the *Polozhenie* statute was abrogated.

Following the decimation and deportation of the Armenian population of Cilicia during 1915-1920, the patriarchal see at Sis was confiscated by the Turkish authorities. In 1929, with the help of the Armenian Patriarchate of Jerusalem, Catholicos Sahak II of Cilicia eventually established his seat at Antelias, north of Beirut, Lebanon, under the French mandate.

The Armenian Church became a member of the World Council of Churches in 1963.

His Holiness Vasken, Catholicos of All Armenians, visited His Holiness Pope Paul VI at the Vatican in 1970.

Following the breakup of the Soviet Union and the proclamation of the independence of the Republic of Armenia (September 1991), the Mother See of Holy Etchmiadzin has been facing the awesome challenge of redefining the role and mission of the Armenian Church within the territories of the former Soviet Union. Freedom of worship having now been guaranteed for citizens of Armenia, the hierarchy of the Armenian Church is concerned about the need to prepare large cadres of properly trained clergy, to organize religious education for all ages of worshipers, to initiate and encourage charitable and social service activities, to promote fund raising for the restoration of hundreds of ruined or closed churches and monasteries and for the construction of new cathedrals and parish churches, and to eventually undo the damage caused by proselytizing foreign missionaries.

Distinctive Features and Teaching

The hierarchical center of the Armenian Church is at Holy Etchmiadzin, Armenia. His Holiness Catholicos and Supreme Patriarch Karekin I is the 131st pontiff since St. Gregory the Enlightener.

Candidates to the priesthood may be chosen from among married men, but marriage may not follow ordination. Celibate priests are required to make a perpetual vow. Candidates for the episcopate must be celibate. The Supreme Patriarch Catholicos is elected in a General Assembly composed of clerical and lay delegates from all the dioceses and the patriarchates.

There are four seminaries, located at Holy Etchmiadzin, Bikfaya (Lebanon), Jerusalem, and New Rochelle, New York (under the name of St. Nersess, administered by the Eastern and Western Dioceses of the Church in the USA and the Canadian Diocese).

Communion is administered under both species by intinction, with the priest placing a broken portion of the wafer soaked in wine on the tongue of the communicant. The wafer is unleavened bread, baked by the priest on the day of the liturgy. It is circular in form and stamped with the sign of the cross. The wine must be undiluted by water. The divine liturgy is chanted in classical Armenian, with priest, deacon, and choir participating.

By an encyclical of Catholicos Gevorg V, dated November 9, 1922, the Gregorian calendar was introduced everywhere except in the Patriarchate of Jerusalem and in some dioceses of the then Soviet Union. Theophany (Epiphany-Christmas) is still celebrated on January 6 as one unitary feast of the appearance of our Lord in the flesh, according to the ancient tradition of the Eastern Churches. The Armenian calendar is the only one that has kept the original usage, not admitting the separate Western Nativity celebration on December 25. The festive period lasts until January 13, culminating in the Feast of the Naming of Jesus Christ.

The North American Situation

In 1889, the first Armenian parish in North America was organized by Fr. Hovsep Sarajian in Worcester, Massachusetts. He was sent by the Armenian Patriarchate of Constantinople at the request of Armenian immigrants residing in Massachusetts.

In 1898, the Diocese of the Armenian Church of America was established by order of His Holiness Catholicos Mkrtich Khrimian. He consecrated Fr. Hovsep Sarajian a bishop and sent him to America as the first diocesan primate. Headquarters were set up at the Church of Our Savior in Worcester.

The diocesan headquarters of the Eastern Diocese of the Armenian Church of America have been located in New York City since 1927 when they were transferred from Massachusetts. St. Vartan's Cathedral, consecrated in 1968 by His Holiness Catholicos Vasken I, constitutes part of the diocesan complex at 630 Second Avenue, New York, N.Y. The California parishes were formed into a separate diocese in 1928, and the Canadian region became a diocese in 1984.

The geographic areas of concentration in the United States are eastern Massachusetts and Rhode Island, metropolitan New York-New Jersey, Philadelphia and vicinity, greater Detroit, Chicago and its suburbs, and four areas in California: San Joaquin Valley, San Fernando Valley, Los Angeles and vicinity, and the San Francisco Bay area. In Canada the faithful are concentrated in Toronto and Montreal.

There are roughly 800,000 communicants in North America.

Dues-paying adult members are estimated to number 25,000, not including those who belong to the separate jurisdiction in the United States under the Patriarchate of Cilicia.

There are 90 clergymen (bishops and priests), not including those in the United States and Canada under the Patriarchate of Cilicia.

The official periodical of the Eastern Diocese is *The Armenian Church*, a bimonthly magazine predominantly in English. The monthly publication of the Western Diocese is *The Mother Church*, an eight-page tabloid that includes two pages in Armenian.

THE COPTIC ORTHODOX CHURCH

by Reverend Gabriel A. Abdelsayed[2]

The Name of the Church
The Coptic Orthodox Church is also known as the Church of Alexandria, the capital of Egypt during the Greco-Roman period. The word "Copt" derives from the "gypt" in *Aigypptos*, the Greek word for Egyptian.

Historical Origins
The Copts pride themselves in the apostolic origin of their Church, which was founded by St. Mark the Evangelist. He is regarded as the first of the 117 patriarchs of Alexandria, as well as the first of many Egyptian saints and glo-

---

[2] Fr. Abdelsayed died on December 2, 1993. This article has been updated by the Coptic delegate to the National Council of Churches.

rious martyrs. St. Mark is believed to have come to Alexandria between the years 48 and 55. His first convert was named Anianus, whom he later ordained bishop to be his successor, together with three priests and seven deacons. St. Jerome states that St. Mark established the School of Alexandria, which became the highest center of theological education in the Middle East. He was martyred in the year 68. He was buried under the altar of a church, but Venetian merchants took the headless body of St. Mark to Venice in 828, while the head remained under the altar in Alexandria. In 1968, thanks to the good relations between Coptic Pope Kyrillos VI and Pope Paul VI, a part of his relics was returned from Venice and buried under the altar of the new Coptic Cathedral in Cairo.

Major Turning Points in History

The Coptic Church was subjected to various persecutions under the Romans from 68 to 639.

So profound was the impression of the persecution of Diocletian on Coptic life that the Copts date their Calendar of the Martyrs from this epoch; the first year of this calendar, A.M. 1 (*Anno Martyri*), is 284, the disastrous year of the accession of Diocletian.

In 312, Constantine the Great's edict of toleration ushered in the triumph of Christianity over paganism and the reversal of the policy of persecution. Old pagan temples were transformed into Christian churches. Christianity became the state religion in 381.

Despite this long period of Roman persecution, Alexandrian Christianity was renowned for its saints, the Fathers of the Coptic Church, and the great theologians of the School of Alexandria (Pantaenus, Clement of Alexandria, Origen).

The first great name to emerge as the head of the school was Pantaenus (d. 190). He was succeeded by Clement, who was followed in about 215 by his brilliant student Origen, one of the greatest exegetical scholars of all time. After his discord with Patriarch Demetrius, the school came under the direct control of the patriarchal and church authority. Origen's immediate successor was Heracles, his former pupil and assistant, who later succeeded Demetrius on the see of St. Mark from 230 to 246. It is said that when he increased the number of local bishops to twenty, the presbyters of the Church decided to distinguish him from the rest of the bishops by calling him "pope," a common title for bishops of Alexandria from the third to the fifth centuries. Among the most reputed scholars who headed the school was Dionysius of Alexandria, later surnamed "the Great" (Patriarch from 246 to 264). His successor was Didymus the Blind (265 to 298). The school played a crucial role in shaping Christian doctrine and theological scholarship during the first four centuries.

The attempt to eradicate heresy and doctrinal differences among the various centers of Christianity bore fruit in the first three ecumenical councils of Nicea (325), Constantinople (381), and Ephesus (431). Two spiritual and intellectual leaders of the Coptic Church, St. Athanasius and St. Cyril of Alexandria, played predominant roles at these councils.

Beginning in the fourth century, Pentapolis, Nubia, and Ethiopia were recognized as being under the jurisdiction of the See of St. Mark.

Coptic monasticism was a gift of Egypt to Christendom. From its modest beginnings on the edge of the desert, it developed into a way of life that was a wonder to Christian antiquity. Most writers ascribe the origins of monasticism to St. Anthony (c. 295-373), whose fame was spread by St. Athanasius' *Life of Saint Anthony*. Pachomius (d. 346) introduced the cenobitic system in 290.

Following their rejection of the Council of Chalcedon, the Copts suffered fierce persecution at the hands of the Chalcedonians.

After the Arab conquest of Egypt in 640, the Copts continued their unwavering loyalty to their Church and to the faith of their forefathers.

The Copts had to give up many material privileges in order to retain their spiritual heritage. Before the Crusades, however, they adapted themselves to the conditions of Islamic rule without the loss of their way of life, and were generally accepted and often esteemed by the caliphs. They were the clerks, tax collectors, and treasurers of the caliphate, and they seemed able to make themselves indispensable to the civil service. The Crusades antagonized the Moslems toward all "worshipers of the Cross," whether Latin, Greek, or Coptic, and the difficulties of the Copts remained acute under both the Mamluk and Ottoman regimes (twelfth to eighteenth centuries).

During the French occupation of Egypt (1798-1801) and the reign of Muhammed Ali (1805-1850), the situation improved. Copts were widely used in the administration and some rose to high office.

In 1959, under the late Pope Kyrillos VI, there began a renaissance of all aspects of Church life that is still very much in progress under the present Pope Shenouda III.

In 1973, Pope Shenouda III visited Pope Paul VI. They signed a Common Declaration stating that in the essence of the faith (including christology) the two Churches are one. But they recognized differences in some dogmas and rituals, and they encouraged theologians to study ways to reconcile them.

The Coptic Church is a member of the World Council of Churches, the United States National Council of Churches, and the All-Africa Council of Churches.

Distinctive Features and Teaching
Cairo, Egypt, is the hierarchical center of the See of St. Mark. The present Pope Shenouda III, "Pope of Alexandria and Patriarch of the See of St. Mark," is the 117th successor of St. Mark. He presides over all the clergy and faithful.

Candidates for the priesthood may be chosen from among married men. Marriage may not follow ordination, even if the priest's wife dies. Monks must be celibate. A monk is eligible for promotion to all ranks of the priesthood, including patriarch.

The Coptic Orthodox Church has one seminary located in Cairo, with seven branches in seven dioceses in Egypt.

The holy Eucharist is administered under both species. The holy bread (*Korban*) is leavened and is prepared for the divine liturgy celebrated on the same day. It is circular in form, with a round stamp bearing the sign of the cross and the *Trisagion*. The wine must be fresh and undiluted. In Egypt, the divine liturgy is celebrated in both Coptic and Arabic. In countries of the diaspora, both Coptic and the local vernacular are used. Priests, deacons, and the people all have their particular part in the service.

The Copts repudiate the identification of Alexandrian Christianity with the Eutychian heresy, which declared the complete absorption of Christ's humanity into his single divine nature. Copts clearly uphold St. Cyril's doctrine of the two natures—divine and human—mystically united in one, without confusion, mingling, or alteration.

The Coptic Church still uses her own ecclesiastical calendar, the Calendar of the Martyrs (see above). Christmas, celebrated according to the Julian calendar, falls on January 7 in the Gregorian calendar.

The North American Situation
In 1965, the first parish was organized by Fr. Marcos Marcos in Toronto, Canada.

The Diocese of North America was established in 1965, with His Holiness the pope as its immediate bishop.

In 1969, Fr. Bishoy Kamal established a Coptic Orthodox parish in Los Angeles, California.

In 1970, Fr. Gabriel Abdelsayed established a Coptic Orthodox parish in New Jersey (St. Mark's).

Geographic areas of concentration are metropolitan New York-New Jersey, Washington, D.C., Los Angeles, San Francisco, Chicago, Troy (Michigan), Cleveland, Houston, Philadelphia, Toronto, and Montreal.

There are roughly 150,000 communicants in the United States, and 50,000 in Canada. Each parish church has its own periodical, published mainly in English and Arabic.

Altogether there are 51 churches in the United States and 15 in Canada.

THE ETHIOPIAN ORTHODOX CHURCH

by Archbishop Yesehaq

The Name of the Church
The Ethiopian Orthodox Church is also known as the Ethiopian Orthodox *Tewahedo* Church. The word *Tewahedo*, which means "made one," was chosen to profess the one nature of Our Lord Jesus Christ.

Historical Origins
The Ethiopian Orthodox Church, indigenous to Africa, is both one of the oldest Churches in the world and a founding member of the World Council of Churches. The Church was the creator of Ethiopia's arts, crafts, and literature, as well as the secular and theological educational institutions. Until the time of Emperor Menelik II, the Church was responsible for educating the nation. Even the *Fetha Nagast* ("The Law of the Kings"), which comprises both canon and civil law, is the creation of the Church.

Ethiopia was the first African nation to worship the one true God of the Old Testament. This was officially established by Queen Makeda on return from her historic visit to King Solomon in Jerusalem. Their union produced King Menelik I. The ancient *Kebra Nagast* ("The Glory of the Kings") states that when Menelik grew up he visited his father Solomon in Jerusalem, and returned home accompanied by Azarias, the son of Zadok the High Priest, and many other Israelites. They carried with them the Ark of the Covenant, and placed it in St. Mary of Zion Church in Axum, the birthplace of Ethiopian civilization.

Ethiopia embraced Christianity and has maintained its doctrines from the era of the apostles to the present day. Acts 8:26-39 recounts the story of the Ethiopian eunuch who was baptized by St. Philip. This eunuch was a minister of Candace, Queen of Ethiopia. This story is the beginning of Ethiopian church history. Eusebius speaks of this eunuch as the first fruits of the faith in the whole world. Irenaeus writes that he preached the Gospel to the Ethiopians. Tradition further records that the apostle Matthew preached the Gospel to the Ethiopians and won a few converts to the new doctrine before leaving the country.

The book of St. Tekle Haimanot recounts that in the beginning of the fourth century, Meropius, a pilgrim from Tyre, came to Ethiopia accompanied by two young men, Frumentius and Aedesius, both Christians. They were received graciously by Anbaram the High Priest. Meropius fell ill and died, but the two young men remained in Ethiopia. Later, Frumentius was chosen to go to Alexandria, where Patriarch Athanasius consecrated him bishop and sent him back to Axum. He was known there as Abba Selama, "Father of Peace."

According to some historians, the introduction of Christianity to Ethiopia was during the reign of King Ezana (320-256), the first African king to become a Christian and make Christianity the official religion of his empire.

Nine Syrian saints who came to Ethiopia in the fifth century also made a large contribution to the growth of the Church by translating books from Greek, Hebrew, Syriac, and other tongues into the classical Ethiopian language of Geez and by propagating the Gospel, as well as founding monasteries and schools.

Major Turning Points in History

For centuries the Christian Ethiopians fought for the maintenance of the Christian faith against internal and external foes.

In 968, a Jewish persecution of Christians occurred under Yodit (Judith).

Later, there was constant hostility from the Muslims of the Red Sea coast. In 1528, Ahmed Gran, a Muslim, attacked the country with the aid of Turkish troops. For over a decade innumerable monasteries and churches were sacked and burned, and ancient manuscripts and other works of art were stolen.

The third and greatest problem was the attempt of the Roman Catholic Church from 1520 to 1631 to bring the Ethiopian Christians under the jurisdiction of Rome. Several missionaries were sent to proselytize as a result of contacts with King Manuel and King Joam of Portugal, initiated by Empress Eleni and her son Lebna Dengel of Ethiopia. They desired to fortify their country against the Turkish menace by making an alliance with a Christian power, and to protect the Holy Land. Among the notable missionaries was Pedro Pais, who reached Ethiopia in 1603 and converted Emperor Susneyos of Ethiopia to the Catholic faith.

Pedro Pais ordered the people to kneel to him as representative of the pope. Priests of the Ethiopian Church had to be reordained by him, and the whole population of the country was regarded as heathen if not rebaptized in the Catholic faith. Churches had to be reconstructed and altars rebuilt in the Portuguese fashion. Meanwhile, Susneyos decreed the death penalty for those who refused to accept the Chalcedonian formula of 451, which the Ethiopians had rejected. The people revolted, civil war broke out, and thousands were killed. After Susneyos died in 1631, his son Fasilades expelled the Jesuit missionaries from the country.

After the mission of the Portuguese Jesuits ended, several christological formulas emerged, two of which were *Qebat* (Anointing) and *Tsegga* (Son of Grace). *Qebat* states that Jesus became perfect man and perfect God by the anointing of the Holy Spirit in the Jordan River, and not at the Incarnation. *Tsegga* professes three births: the Son's eternal birth from the Father, the Son's genetic birth from the Virgin Mary, and his birth from the Holy Spirit during baptism. These teachings caused great controversy and division in the Church, especially during the reign of Emperor Tewodros II (1855-1868). Such doctrinal formulas were stamped out by decree of Emperor Tewodros and by Yohanness IV, who succeeded him.

Another attempt at proselytism was made during the Italian occupation under Mussolini (1935-1940).

From the beginning, the Ethiopian Church was affiliated with the See of St. Mark of Alexandria. After the death of Frumentius, the first bishop of Ethiopia, Egyptian Coptic bishops were appointed to head the Ethiopian Church. This continued until early in the twentieth century. However, numerous problems such as language and distance from Alexandria made it imperative to have native bishops, and after a long period of struggle beginning in 1926, agreement was finally reached with the Coptic Patriarchate in 1950. Abuna Basilios, an Ethiopian, was consecrated metropolitan.

In 1959, the Church of Ethiopia was granted autocephaly (full independence), while remaining in canonical union with the Coptic Church. This granting of autocephaly was crowned on April 6, 1971. On that day the See of Addis Ababa was elevated to patriarchal rank, and Abuna Theophilus was elected Patriarch in Addis Ababa.

Distinctive Features and Teaching

The Church teaches the Five Pillars of Mystery: the trinity, incarnation, baptism, Eucharist, and the resurrection of the dead. These mysteries are regarded as basic by the Church, and every Christian must know them.

The first three ecumenical councils are accepted, but not the Council of Chalcedon (451), which teaches the formula of the two natures against the one nature teaching of St. Cyril of Alexandria. The Ethiopian Church holds that they were two natures before the Incarnation, but only one after the union. The human nature was not dissolved in the divine as Eutyches taught, but rather, the divine made the human nature immediately its own, and union is established without confusion and without division. The Church rejects the teaching of Eutyches, which was regarded by Chalcedonian theologians to be the same as the teachings of the Ethiopian Church and its sister Churches. The Church emphasizes that all concerning Christ should be applied to his entire person as one Lord, and not to single out the "human nature" as subject to suffering, hunger, passion, etc. Properties peculiar to the human are referred to his divine powers, since God suffered, God was crucified, etc.

The hierarchical center of the Ethiopian Orthodox Church is the Holy Synod in Addis Ababa, Ethiopia. His Holiness Abuna Paulos is the present patriarch.

The patriarch is first nominated by the Holy Synod and then elected by delegates representing the whole Ethiopian Church. The election is administered by a committee appointed by the Synod.

In the Ethiopian Church, there are both married and celibate priests. If one wishes to marry, he must do so prior to becoming a priest. Celibate priests are required to make a perpetual vow, and only celibate priests can be elevated to the episcopate.

The eucharistic bread must be made of pure wheat flour to which nothing is added save water and leaven. It must be baked not earlier than three hours before the beginning of the liturgy. The wine is prepared from dried raisins. These are soaked in water for three to five hours and the juice is squeezed out into vessels where it remains until transferred to the chalice at the time of the service.

The services are conducted in Geez and Amharic, and in the Western Hemisphere English is also used. There are two distinct orders in the service of the Church: (1) the priests and deacons who officiate at the Mass, and (2) the *debteras*, or master cantors, whose duties entail executing the liturgical chants.

The Church follows the Julian calendar. The Nativity of Christ is celebrated on January 7 in the Gregorian reckoning.

Every monastery in Ethiopia has its own traditional church school or seminary. A few of the most popular are Holy Trinity Theological College, St. Paul Theological Seminary, and Menelik II School in Addis Ababa; and St. Yared Theological Seminary and Abraha and Asbaha in Tigre Province.

The North American Situation

In 1959, the Church was first established concurrently in New York, Trinidad, and Guyana by the late Patriarch, His Holiness Abuna Theophilus, who at that time was the Archbishop of Harar Province in Ethiopia.

An Ethiopian Orthodox Diocese for the entire Western Hemisphere was established in 1972. The geographic areas of concentration in North America are Bronx (New York), California, Toronto, Bermuda, and the West Indies. In all the churches of the Western Hemisphere there are about 90,000 communicants, comprising both Western-born and Ethiopians.

Editor's Note:

Since this article was written, there have been several important developments in the life of the Ethiopian Orthodox Church. The Marxist revolution in 1974 overthrew Emperor Haile Selasse and officially separated the Church from the state. This marked the beginning of a period of vigorous persecution of all religions in the country. In 1976 the government deposed Patriarch Theophilos and arrested him. It was revealed in 1992 that he had been murdered in prison in 1979.

Following the collapse of the communist government in May 1991, Patriarch Merkorios (elected 1988) was accused of collaboration with the Marxist regime. Under pressure, he resigned as Patriarch in September. On July 5, 1992, the Holy Synod elected Abuna Paulos as fifth Patriarch of the Ethiopian Orthodox Church. Later, Patriarch Merkorios challenged the election of Paulos and demanded that he be reinstated in office.

In the United States, Ethiopian Orthodox Archbishop Yesehaq did not recognize the election of Paulos and broke communion with the Patriarchate in 1992. The Holy Synod then decided to divide the Archdiocese of the Western Hemisphere into three jurisdictions, and appointed Archbishop Matthias as new Bishop of the United States and Canada. This caused a split in the American Ethiopian Orthodox community which, as of mid-1995, had not yet been resolved.

THE SYRIAN ORTHODOX CHURCH OF ANTIOCH

by Very Reverend Chorepiscopus John Meno

The Name of the Church

The Syrian Orthodox Church of Antioch is also called the Syrian Jacobite Church (see below).

The Patriarchate of Antioch claims the greatest antiquity of all the Churches of Christendom. Acts 11:26 confirms that the disciples were first called Christians in Antioch. According to tradition, St. Peter established the See of Antioch, presiding over it prior to his departure for the West. The Patriarchate of Antioch held ecclesiastical authority over all the territory between the Mediterranean Sea and the Persian Gulf, a jurisdiction confirmed by both the Council of Nicea (325) and the Council of Constantinople (381). Later, this authority was to spread even as far as India and China through the Church's missionary endeavors.

Major Turning Points in History

Around the beginning of the fourth century, the Catholicate of the East was established at Seleucia-Ctesiphon, comprising the bishoprics within the Persian Empire and Mesopotamia. This Catholicate eventually fell victim to Persian political persecution and Nestorianism. In 628, a new Catholicate was established in Mesopotamia by Patriarch Athanasius I and was soon expanded to include all Arabia, Persia, and Afghanistan. It lasted until 1859. In 1964, Patriarch Ignatius Yacoub III approved the establishment of the Catholicate of the East in India.

The Syrian Orthodox Church of Antioch participated in and accepts the Ecumenical Councils of Nicea (325), Constantinople (381), and Ephesus (431), but rejected the decisions of the Council of Chalcedon (451), specifically concerning its interpretation of the two natures of Christ. Due to this, and to political oppression, the Syrian Orthodox Church of Antioch was to undergo many persecutions and hardships.

In 518, Patriarch Severus was forced into exile and established his residence in Egypt, where he labored to keep the Syrian Church of Antioch alive. By 544, only three bishops remained free to serve the needs of the Church. During this critical period, a dedicated monk, Jacob Baradaeus, won the support and protection of Empress Theodora, was consecrated as a general metropolitan by Patriarch Theodosius of Alexandria, and was authorized to restore the persecuted Churches of the Patriarchates of Antioch and Alexandria. Assisted by three fellow bishops, Mor Jacob visited the faithful throughout the entire Middle East, Asia Minor, and even Ethiopia, rebuilding and expanding the Church. Tradition says he ordained over 100,000 priests, 27 bishops, and one Patriarch of Antioch, Paul II. Due to Mor Jacob's efforts, the Syrian Orthodox Church is often referred to as the Syrian "Jacobite" Church.

On the eve of the Muslim conquest, the Syrian Orthodox Church of Antioch was once again a victim of Byzantine persecution. Constantinople recognized only the Byzantine (Melkite) Patriarch of Antioch. The early years of Muslim occupation were characterized by religious tolerance and justice, and the Syrian Orthodox enjoyed positions of great influence and prestige under the Caliphs. During this period, the Arabs were to profit from the culture and learning of the Syrian Church of Antioch.

Following the Crusades, religious toleration gave way to alienation and open persecution.

This situation was further aggravated by the Mongol invasions. The coming of Timur Lane was to spell slaughter and devastation for the Syrian Orthodox Church.

In 1236, the Syrian Orthodox Church of Antioch numbered about 20,000 parishes, not to mention hundreds of monasteries and convents. The Church also had great educational and cultural institutions, including the famous schools of Antioch, Nusaybin, and Edessa, and eminent scholars. The tragedies and difficulties already mentioned were to bring an end to the growth and cultural achievements of the Syrian Church.

The situation was further aggravated in the following years by divisions resulting from missionary endeavors, first by Roman Catholic and later by Protestant missionaries.

The coming of the First World War was to bring renewed persecution in Turkey, with large numbers of Syrian Orthodox being forced to flee as refugees into various parts of the Arab Middle East.

Distinctive Features and Teaching

The patriarchate is located in Damascus, Syria. His Holiness Moran Mor Ignatius Zakka I, elevated in 1980, is the 121st Patriarch of Antioch and All the East and the Supreme Head of the Universal Syrian Orthodox Church. The Church numbers about two million faithful who reside principally in the Middle East, India, and the Americas, with growing communities in both Europe and Australia. The Church operates parochial schools, theological seminaries, hospitals, and orphanages in the Middle East and India, and is active in such ecclesiastical bodies as the World Council of Churches and the National Council of Churches of Christ in the United States.

Candidates for episcopal consecration are selected from the monastic clergy and are consecrated by His Holiness the Patriarch, assisted by at least two metropolitans. The patriarch is elected to the throne by the Holy Synod, which is composed of the Church's metropolitans.

The official language of the Church is Syriac.

Though the official calendar of the Church is the Julian, the Church in India now observes Easter according to the Gregorian date.

The basic beliefs of the Syrian Orthodox Church of Antioch are based on Holy Scripture and embodied in the Nicene Creed.

The Church professes that Christ is of one nature and that he is indivisible into two natures, being fully God and fully man in the unique oneness of his person and nature, without mixture or confusion. Christ's true Godhead and his humanity were essentially united at his Incarnation.

The Holy Spirit is confessed to proceed from the Father and to be the giver of life to all.

Syrian Orthodox profess Mary to be truly the Bearer of God (*Yoldath Aloho*). The Church acknowledges the purity and virginity of Mary not only before, but also during and after the birth of Jesus.

The Church professes the faith of the three Ecumenical Councils of Nicea, Constantinople, and Ephesus. The Syrian Orthodox Church of Antioch condemns Eutychianism, which affirmed the one nature in Christ, but only one of divinity, not humanity. The Syrian Church has always professed Christ to be both truly God and fully man, but in one united and unique nature.

Syrian Orthodox faithful profess that Jesus Christ entrusted the holy Church to the apostles, and most specifically to St. Peter, Chief of the Apostles. The Church accepts apostolic succession and looks upon the Syrian Orthodox Patriarch of Antioch and All the East as the true successor to St. Peter the Apostle, the first Patriarch of the Holy See of Antioch, acknowledging His Holiness as the Supreme Head of the Universal Syrian Orthodox Church and as seated upon the Throne of St. Peter of the Holy See of Antioch.

North American Situation

The presence of Syrian Orthodox in North America dates back to the late nineteenth century, when faithful started to emigrate from Turkey to the United States and Canada. Syrian faithful from Diyarbekir, Turkey, qualified as workers in silk, settled in New Jersey, a major center of the silk industry. Families from Harput, Turkey, were drawn to Massachusetts, while faithful from the Turkish province of Tur 'Abdin, being chiefly weavers by trade, established themselves in Rhode Island as employees in the local weaving mills. Families from Mardin, Turkey, were to settle in Quebec, Canada, during the same period. Meanwhile, Syrian Orthodox from villages near Homs, Syria, journeyed to the United States to settle in and around Detroit, Michigan.

On May 20, 1907, Hanna Koorie was ordained a priest for the Syrian Orthodox families in the United States.

In the 1920s, parishes were established in Worcester, Massachusetts, Central Falls, Rhode Island, and West New York, New Jersey.

On January 29, 1949, His Eminence Mar Athanasius Yeshue Samuel, then Syrian Orthodox Metropolitan of Jerusalem, arrived in the United States and immediately began to tend to the spiritual needs of the Syrian Orthodox faithful in North America. On May 13, 1952, Archbishop Samuel was appointed patriarchal vicar to the United States and Canada, and on November 15, 1957, His Eminence became Archbishop of the Syrian Orthodox Church in the United States and Canada.

On September 7, 1958, Archbishop Samuel consecrated a cathedral in the name of St. Mark, in Hackensack, New Jersey. In 1980, a new archdiocesan residence was obtained at 49 Kipp Avenue in Lodi, New Jersey. On April 17, 1994, a new cathedral complex was officially opened in Teaneck, New Jersey.

The Archdiocese of the Syrian Orthodox Church in the United States and Canada now has 18 official parishes and four mission congregations.

The archdiocese currently numbers approximately 30,000 communicants, under the jurisdiction of the archbishop, and is presently served by 17 priests, with six retired pastors.

THE SYRIAN CHURCH OF MALABAR

by Very Reverend Dr. K. M. Simon

The Name of the Church
The Syrian Church of Malabar is also known as the Syrian Orthodox Church of India.

Historical Origins
The early history of this Church is shrouded in obscurity. However, tradition assigns the founding of the Christian Church in India to the apostle Thomas, according to the apocryphal *Acts of Judas Thomas*, ascribed to the Edessene writer Bardesanes (154-222). St. Thomas is said to have preached the Gospel, and to have founded seven churches on the coast before going to the opposite side of the subcontinent. Later, he traveled as far as Peking. On his return, he was martyred in Mylapore near Madras. The place of his martyrdom and burial is preserved and today is a place of pilgrimage.

This tradition was never seriously challenged until 1892, when Dr. Milne Rae put forward the theory that the Malabar Church was the product of the Nestorian missionary activity of the fifth and sixth centuries. And, indeed, there were several colonizations from the Middle East to South India in the fourth and fifth centuries.

148

Major Turning Points in History

Around 345, a group of Christians from Mesopotamia, under the leadership of Thomas of Kana, settled in Kerala with their bishop.

In 840, Mar Sabar Isho and Mar Peroz, two Nestorian bishops, arrived with more Syrian emigrants. Hospitable Hindu rulers welcomed them and gave them charters, as had been done previously, granting them a lofty place in their caste system. Their metropolitans were even given civil and ecclesiastical jurisdiction over the community.

During its history, the Church has suffered owing to secessions from it to other Churches. Some of the foreign bishops who came to Malabar were Nestorians. This accounts for the existence of the East Syrian Church in Trichur, which has a membership of over 10,000, and traces of Nestorian doctrine.

When the Portuguese arrived in the sixteenth century, they were surprised to find over 100 churches, which they then sought to bring under Rome. In 1599, their archbishop convened a synod at Diamper, imposing the Roman doctrine and supremacy of the pope. Because of canonical irregularities and abuses, this synod was never approved by Rome.

In 1653, when they heard of the murder of Bishop Athella, who had been sent by the Patriarch of Antioch, some of the faithful assembled at the "leaning cross" in Mattachery Cochin and took an oath, renouncing Rome and returning to their original faith. They had no bishop, so they chose Thomas Pakalomattam to be their prelate, as Mar Thoma I. Conscious that he had no apostolic succession, Mar Thoma wrote to the Patriarch of Antioch to get his elevation regularized, and in 1655 Mar Gregorious came to consecrate Mar Thoma as bishop. Nine bishops with the title Mar Thoma—all members of the same family—presided over the Syrian Church in India until 1817.

In 1813, a seminary was built at Kottayam for the education of the Syrian Christians. Three Anglican missionaries helped to staff the seminary without interfering in matters of faith.

Later, missionaries did not show the same ecumenical spirit, and started interfering in matters of faith, advocating "reforms." This caused a deep split. Some followed the missionaries and formed the C. M. S. Church in Travancore and Cochin, now a part of the Church of South India. Others, headed by their leader Abraham Malpan, revolted against such cherished beliefs and church practices as prayers for the departed, the intercession of Mary and the saints, etc. They also encouraged priests to marry. These groups, first known as "Reformed Syrian Christians," were the forerunners of the Mar Thoma Church which is now in full communion with the Anglicans.

In 1876, Patriarch Peter III of Antioch came to Malabar. He convened a synod at Mulanthuruthy where the faith of the Church was reaffirmed, divided the Church into seven dioceses, and consecrated bishops for each.

In 1910, Patriarch Abdulla visited the Malabar Church. Unfortunately, at this time a controversy arose with regard to matters of discipline and temporalities of the Church. This resulted in the excommunication of Mar Dionysius VI, the then Metropolitan of Malabar. This caused a division in the Church of Malabar, one side remaining loyal to the Patriarch of Antioch and the other declaring themselves to be a totally independent Church under a catholicos. Basalios Mar Thoma I, the first Catholicos of the independent group, was consecrated by Patriarch Abdul Messiah, who had been removed from the patriarchal throne by the synod in Syria. In spite of the split, which still exists, the faith of the Church remains inviolate among the faithful of both groups.

Many attempts at reconciliation, including one by Lord Irwin, then the Viceroy of India, were made without success. In 1957 Mar Ignatius Yacoub II become the Patriarch of Antioch, and in 1958 he recognized the Catholicos as an expression of his sincere desire for reconciliation. In 1964, after the death of the Catholicos, the Patriarch visited Malabar with a retinue of bishops and consecrated Mar Basalius Augen I as the Catholicos of the East. This brought a temporary end to the long division, but now the Church is again split. Today the Church of Malabar has two Catholicoi, one loyal to the Patriarch and the other declaring total independence. Both of them tenaciously hold on to the sacred heritage and faith inherited from their forefathers. The autonomous Church under the Syrian Patriarch is known as "The Malankara Syrian Orthodox Church," while the fully independent group is called "The Malankara Orthodox Syrian Church." The faithful are almost equally divided—about one and one-half million in each group, with the patriarchal party slightly higher. The energy of this dynamic and progressive people in Kerala is thus dissipated. Hope still persists for their eventual reconciliation.

Distinctive Features and Teaching

Although affiliated to the Syrian Orthodox Patriarch of Antioch in its ecclesiastical orders, discipline, doctrine, etc., and an integral part of the Oriental Orthodox world, in communion with all the Oriental Orthodox Churches described in this book, this is, at the same time, a fully indigenous Church. One main weakness is that the faithful have inherited from the Hindus the caste mentality, with its social exclusiveness, and, consequently, there has been practically no missionary or evangelical work among the noncaste Hindus. Had the faithful of this Church been more purposeful, not only would present and previous splits have been avoided, but a good part of India might have been brought to Christ. ~

APPENDIX D

A Glossary of Ecclesiastical Terms Used in This Book

by Reverend Aelred Cody, OSB

Annulment. A juridical declaration that an apparently valid marriage was in fact null and void from the beginning. See also *dissolution.*

Canonical form. The Catholic Church's term for the requirements established for the celebration of a wedding if the marriage is to be valid. The Roman (Latin) Catholic Church requires that a marriage be contracted in the presence (1) of the bride or the groom's diocesan bishop or pastor (or a priest or deacon delegated by the bishop or pastor, or, in exceptional circumstances, even a delegated layperson), who assists at the marriage and receives the contractual promises, and (2) of two other persons who witness the ceremony. The Eastern Catholic Churches have basically the same requirements, but in addition they, like the Orthodox Churches, require a sacred rite which may be celebrated only by a bishop or a priest, not by a deacon or a layperson as in the Latin Church. The Eastern Catholic Churches admit a valid and licit marriage before witnesses alone in exceptional circumstances, but require that the spouses in such a marriage receive the nuptial blessing as soon as possible from a priest. In the Catholic Church, both Western and Eastern, the observance of the canonical form is required for the validity of a marriage in which one or both parties are Catholic, unless the non-Catholic party is Orthodox and the marriage is celebrated according to Orthodox form. The marriage of an Orthodox to a Catholic according to Orthodox form since 1965, if the Catholic is Eastern (the dates of the decrees in 1965 vary among the Eastern Catholic Churches), and since March 25, 1967, if the Catholic is Latin, is considered valid and sacramental in Catholic law. But for such a marriage to be lawful for the Catholic party, he or she must still ask for a dispensation from observance of the canonical form. See also *form.*

Catholicos. Originally this title was used to indicate the "general" status of certain bishops who were, nevertheless, subordinate to a Patriarch. In some cases this is still true today, as for instance the Catholicos of the Malankara Syrian Orthodox Church in India who is subordinate to the Syrian Orthodox

Patriarch in Damascus. But it is now also used in combination with the title Patriarch to indicate the head of a self-governing Church, as for example the head of the Armenian Orthodox Church, the Supreme Patriarch and Catholicos of All Armenians in Etchmiadzin.

Chrismation. In Oriental Orthodox terminology, the anointing with holy chrism oil immediately following the rite of baptism. It is considered an integral part of the rite of Christian initiation that includes the three sacraments of baptism, chrismation, and holy communion. See also *confirmation.*

Christology. The theological interpretation of the mystery of Christ, the eternal Son and Word of God incarnate, perfectly divine, and perfectly human. Christological disagreements between the Oriental Orthodox Churches, which do not accept the decrees of the Council of Chalcedon, and those Churches, including the Roman Church, which have accepted those decrees, have arisen mainly over difficulties in finding satisfactory common understandings of the theological terms person, hypostasis, and nature.

Conciliarity. The principle that major decisions affecting the life, government, and theology of a Church should be made not by a single person or a limited group of persons, but by representatives of all sections of the Church, particularly its bishops, assembled in council, or at least consulted by modern means of communication.

Confirmation. In Roman Catholic terminology, the second sacrament of initiation in which, through the laying on of hands and anointing with oil, the recipient receives the gift of the Holy Spirit. In the Latin Church it is almost always conferred several years after the baptism of an infant. See also *chrismation.*

Consultation. In the United States, a board of persons representing two Churches not in communion with one another, established to deal with issues on which the two Churches have agreed or disagreed, or which are of concern to one or both of them, is often called a *consultation.* In popular speech, such a board is also called a *dialogue,* because its work frequently entails discussion of the positions of both sides, with an effort to arrive at realistic consensus.

Dispensation. A relaxation of a merely ecclesiastical law in a particular case granted by one in authority.

Dissolution. A juridical act by which a valid sacramental marriage is dissolved. In the Oriental Orthodox Churches, a marriage can be dissolved only on grounds of adultery or other very grave grounds which may be specified by a particular Church. In the Catholic Churches, both Western and Eastern, a valid sacramental marriage cannot be dissolved unless it has not been consummated. See also *annulment.*

Eastern Catholic Churches. Churches of an Eastern tradition that are in full communion with the Church of Rome and its bishop. Such Churches have retained their original liturgical, spiritual, and theological traditions basically intact, along with many of their traditional forms of government and practice. All of them are now governed by a single code of canon law which allows the individual Churches to determine certain matters for themselves. Although they are subject to the Pope as head of the college of Catholic bishops, they have a significant level of autonomy. In their ordinary relations with the Church's central authority in Rome, they deal with the Congregation for the Oriental Churches.

Ecclesiology. The theological interpretation of the mystery of the Church and of its forms in this world. Among the issues with which it deals are the government and membership of the Church, the role of the sacraments within it, and the relation of individual Churches with one another.

Exarch. In the Eastern Catholic Churches today, a bishop appointed to govern an ecclesiastical district, usually having few members of the Church in question, which lies outside the territory historically subject to the patriarch or major archbishop of that Church.

Form. The requirements established by ecclesiastical or civil authority for the manner in which a wedding ceremony is to be celebrated if the marriage is to be valid and lawful. The form of the Oriental Orthodox Churches requires that a marriage be blessed by a bishop or a priest according to a sacred rite (a prescribed liturgical form). The Oriental Orthodox admit the validity of a marriage entered into according to Latin Catholic form, but find problematic the Western theological position that the spouses themselves (rather than a bishop or priest celebrating a sacred rite) are the ministers of the sacrament. Eastern Catholic Churches, too, require the blessing of a bishop or priest according to a sacred rite, but they also share the Latin requirements of canonical form insofar as they are not incompatible with Eastern form. See also *canonical form.*

154

Mixed marriage. In the strict sense used throughout this book, a sacramental marriage between validly baptized persons belonging to Churches not in communion with one another. Of the Churches with which this book is concerned, the Armenian Orthodox, Syrian Orthodox, and Roman Catholic Churches admit mixed marriages, with due precaution and the observance of required formalities, while the Coptic Orthodox and Ethiopian Orthodox Churches do not admit them. The Catholic Churches, both Western and Eastern, also allow marriage between a Catholic and a person who is not baptized (an interfaith marriage as opposed to an interchurch one). They accept, in principle, that a marriage between a baptized person and an unbaptized person can be valid. But they do not consider such a marriage sacramental. If the baptized person is a Catholic, the marriage is considered valid only if the Catholic party has first been dispensed from the impediment "of disparity of cult." The Oriental Orthodox Churches do not admit marriage between a baptized person and an unbaptized person.

Oriental Orthodox Churches. By custom, the ancient Eastern Churches not in communion with the bishop of Rome are called Orthodox, while those in communion with him are called Catholic. Of the Orthodox Churches, the Armenian, Coptic, Ethiopian, and Syrian Churches used to be called the "Non-Chalcedonian" or "Pre-Chalcedonian" Churches because they accept only the first three ecumenical councils but not the Council of Chalcedon (451) or subsequent ones. Today these Churches are called Oriental Orthodox to distinguish them from the Eastern Orthodox Churches, which are in communion with the patriarch of Constantinople and accept seven councils as ecumenical.

Patriarch. Originally used to identify the spiritual heads of the five most important Churches (Rome, Constantinople, Alexandria, Antioch, and Jerusalem). In modern times this term is used to identify the supreme hierarchs of the various Eastern and Oriental Orthodox Churches, as well as some of the Eastern Catholic Churches.

Pope. The title, originally the Coptic epithet *papa,* "the father," which is usually used before the name of a Coptic or a Greek Patriarch of Alexandria and of a Patriarch of Rome.

Primacy. The position of a single bishop as first in rank among all bishops of a particular region, or of an entire Church, or of the universal Church. Such a bishop may, or may not, be recognized as having jurisdiction, partial or full, over his entire region or over an entire Church. While many Orthodox Churches recognize the historical primacy of the bishop of Rome, they do not admit the Roman pontiff's universal jurisdiction or primacy as it evolved in the medieval Western Church and was subsequently applied to the Eastern Catholic Churches. The patriarch of each Oriental Orthodox Church (in the Armenian Orthodox Church, the Patriarch and Catholicos of All Armenians at Etchmiadzin) is the supreme primate of his own Church, but the Oriental Orthodox Churches together do not recognize the primacy of one prelate over all of their Churches. In the Catholic Churches the jurisdictional primacy of the bishop of Rome is considered the indispensable condition of communion among local Churches, while in the Oriental Orthodox Churches primacy, at all levels, is not considered primarily a matter of jurisdiction and is seen as a consequence of eucharistic communion and of conciliar agreement within the Church. See also *conciliarity*.

Proselytizing. In contemporary ecumenical discussion, this term refers to activity in which members of one Church attempt to draw converts from another Church with which theirs is not in communion.

APPENDIX E

A Select Bibliography of Books and Essays

GENERAL WORKS

Atiya, Aziz S., *A History of Eastern Christianity*. London: Methuen; Notre Dame, Ind.: University of Notre Dame Press, 1968.

Assfalg, Julius, and Paul Krüger, *Petit dictionnaire de l'orient chrétien*. Maredsous/ Turnhout: Editions Brepols, 1991.

Fries, P. and T. Nersoyan, eds., *Christ in East and West*. Macon, Ga: Mercer University Press, 1987.

Gregorios, P., W. Nazareth, and N. Nissiotis, eds., *Does Chalcedon Divide or Unite? Towards Convergence in Orthodox Christology*. Geneva: World Council of Churches, 1981.

Hill, Henry, *Light from the East: A Symposium on the Oriental Orthodox and Assyrian Churches*. Toronto: Anglican Book Centre, 1988.

Horner, Norman, *A Guide to Christian Churches in the Middle East*. Elkhart, Ind.: Mission Focus, 1989.

Roberson, Ronald, *The Eastern Christian Churches: A Brief Survey*. Rome: Pontifical Oriental Institute, 1993.

THE ARMENIAN ORTHODOX CHURCH

Heyer, Friedrich, ed., *Die Kirche Armeniens*. Die Kirchen der Welt, no. 18. Stuttgart: Evangelisches Verlagswerk, 1978.

Krikorian, Mesrob K., "The Armenian Church in the Soviet Union, 1917-1967." In *Aspects of Religion in the Soviet Union, 1917-1967*, edited by R. H. Marshall, Jr., Thomas E. Bird, and Andrew Q. Blane. Chicago/ London: University of Chicago Press, 1971, 239-256.

Mécérian, Jean, *Histoire et institutions de l'Eglise d'Arménie: Evolution nationale et doctrinale, spiritualité, monachisme*. Recherches publiées sous la direction de l'Institut de Lettres Orientales de Beyrouth, no. 30. Beyrouth: Imprimerie catholique, [1965].

Mouradian, C., "The Armenian Apostolic Church." In *Eastern Christianity and Politics in the Twentieth Century*, edited by P. Ramet. Durham, N.C.: Duke University Press, 1988, 353-374.

Nersoyan, Tiran, *The Divine Liturgy of the Armenian Apostolic Orthodox Church*. New York: Delphic Press, 1950.

Ormanian, Malachia, *The Church of Armenia: Her History, Doctrine, Rule, Discipline, Liturgy, Literature, and Existing Condition*. Translated from the French edition by G. Marcar Gregory, 1912. 2d rev. English ed., 1955. Reprint. New York: St. Vartan Press, 1988.

———, *A Dictionary of the Armenian Church*. Translated by Bedros Norehad. New York: St. Vartan Press, 1984.

Sarkissian, Karekin, "The Armenian Church." In *Religion in the Middle East: Three Religions in Concord and Conflict*, edited by A. J. Arberry. Vol. 1, *Judaism and Christianity*. Cambridge: University Press, 1969, 482-520.

———, *A Brief Introduction to Armenian Christian Literature*. London: Faith Press, 1960.

———, *The Council of Chalcedon and the Armenian Church*. London: Society for Promoting Christian Knowledge, 1965.

THE COPTIC ORTHODOX CHURCH

Atiya, Aziz S., ed., *The Coptic Encyclopedia*. 8 vols. New York: Macmillan, 1991.

Cannuyer, Christian, *Les Coptes*. Collection Fils d'Abraham. Maredsous/ Turnhout: Editions Brepols, 1990.

Khs-Burmester, O. H. E., *The Egyptian or Coptic Church: A Detailed Description of Her Liturgical Services and the Rites and Ceremonies Observed in the Administration of Her Sacraments*. Publications de la Société d'Archéologie Copte, textes et documents, no. 8. Cairo: Société d'Archéologie Copte, 1967.

Cramer, Maria, *Das christlich-koptische Ägypten einst und heute: Eine Orientierung*. Wiesbaden: Otto Harrassowitz, 1959.

Malaty, Tadros Y., *Introduction to the Coptic Orthodox Church*. Sporting-Alexandria, Egypt: St. George's Coptic Orthodox Church (available in North America from the author, 100 West Sixth Street, Second Floor, Bayonne, NJ 07002).

Martin, P., C. Van Nispen, and F. Sidarouss, "Les nouveaux courants dans la communauté copte orthodoxe," *Proche Orient Chrétien* 40 (1990) 245-257.

Meinardus, Otto F. A., *Christian Egypt, Ancient and Modern*. 2d rev. ed. Cairo: American University in Cairo Press, 1977.

———, *Christian Egypt: Faith and Life*. Cairo: American University in Cairo Press, 1970.

————, "The Coptic Church in Egypt." In *Religion in the Middle East: Three Religions in Concord and Conflict*, edited by A. J. Arberry. Vol. 1, Judaism and Christianity. Cambridge: University Press, 1969, 423-453.

"The Roman Catholic Church and the Coptic Orthodox Church: Documents (1973-1988)," a special issue of *Information Service* (Pontifical Council for Promoting Christian Unity) 76 (1991/I).

Wakin, Edward, *A Lonely Minority: The Modern Story of Egypt's Copts*. New York: Morrow, 1963.

Worrell, W. H., *A Short Account of the Copts*. Henry Russel Lecture for 1941-1942. Ann Arbor: University of Michigan Press, 1945.

THE ETHIOPIAN ORTHODOX CHURCH

Bonk, Jon, *An Annotated and Classified Bibliography of English Literature Pertaining to the Ethiopian Orthodox Church*. Metuchen and London: The American Theological Library Association and The Scarecrow Press, 1984.

Hammerschmidt, Ernst, *Studies in the Ethiopic Anaphoras*. Äthiopistische Forschungen, no. 25. 2d rev. ed. Stuttgart: Franz Steiner, 1987.

Heyer, Friedrich, *Die Kirche Äthiopiens: Eine Bestandaufnahme*. Theologische Bibliothek Töpelmann, no. 22. Berlin/New York: Walter de Gruyter, 1971.

Hyatt, Harry Middleton, *The Church of Abyssinia*. London: Luzac, 1928.

Isaac, Ephraim, "An Obscure Component in Ethiopian Church History: An Examination of the Various Theories Pertaining to the Origins and Nature of Ethiopian Christianity," *Le Muséon* 85 (1972) 225-258.

Larebo, H. "The Ethiopian Orthodox Church." In *Eastern Christianity and Politics in the Twentieth Century*, edited by P. Ramet. Durham, N.C.: Duke University Press, 1988, 375-400.

Lößl, Josef, "One as the Same: Elements of an Ethiopian Christology," *Ostkirchliche Studien* 42 (1993) 288-302.

O'Hanlon, Douglas, *Features of the Abyssinian Church*. London: Society for Promoting Christian Knowledge, 1946.

O'Leary, De Lacy, *The Ethiopian Church: Historical Notes on the Church of Abyssinia*. London: Society for Promoting Christian Knowledge, 1936.

Stoffregen-Pedersen, Kirsten, *Les Éthiopiens*. Collection Fils d'Abraham. Maredsous/Turnhout: Editions Brepols, 1990.

The Teaching of the Abyssinian Church as Set Forth by the Doctors of the Same. Translated by the Rev. A. F. Matthew, with an introduction by Canon J.

A. Douglas. London: Faith Press; New York/Milwaukee: Morehouse Publishing Co., 1936.

Uqbit, Tesfazghi, *Current Christological Positions of Ethiopian Orthodox Theologians*. Orientalia Christiana Analecta no. 196. Rome: Pontifical Oriental Institute, 1973.

Yesehaq, Archbishop, *The Ethiopian Tewahedo Church: An Integrally African Church*. New York/Los Angeles/Chicago: Vantage Press, 1989.

THE SYRIAN ORTHODOX CHURCH

Anschütz, Helga, *Die syrischen Christen vom Tur 'Abdin: Eine altchristliche Bevölkerungsgruppe zwischen Beharrung, Stagnation und Auflösung*. Das östliche Christentum, n.s., no. 34. Würzburg: Augustinus-Verlag, 1984.

Codrington, H. W., "The Syrian Liturgy." In *Studies of the Syrian Liturgies*. London: Geo. E. J. Coldwell [1952], 1-47 . (First published in *Eastern Churches Quarterly* 1 [1936] 10-20, 40-49, 87-99, 135-148.)

Dauvillier, Jean, "L'Expansion de l'Église syrienne en asie centrale et en extreme-orient," *L'Orient syrien* 1 (1956) 76-87.

Joseph, John, *Muslim-Christian Relations and Inter-Christian Rivalries in the Middle East: The Case of the Jacobites in an Age of Transition*. Albany: State University of New York Press, 1983.

McCullough, William Stewart, *A Short History of Syriac Christianity to the Rise of Islam*. Chico, Calif.: Scholars Press, 1982.

Palmer, Andrew, *Monk and Mason on the Tigris Frontier: The Early History of Tur 'Abdin*. University of Cambridge Oriental Publications. Cambridge/ New York: Cambridge University Press, 1990.

Ramban Kadavil Paul, *The Orthodox Syrian Church, Its Religion and Philosophy*. Alwaye: Alwaye Press, Friendship House, 1973.

Sélis, Claude, *Les Syriens orthodoxes et catholiques*. Collection Fils d'Abraham. Maredsous/Turnhout: Editions Brepols, 1988.

THE THOMAS CHRISTIANS IN INDIA

Daniel, David, *The Orthodox Church of India*. New Delhi: Miss Rachel David, 1986.

Howard, George Broadley, *The Christians of St. Thomas and Their Liturgies*. 1864. Reprint. Farnborough: Gregg International, 1969.

Kollaparambil, Jacob, *The Babylonian Origin of the Southists Among the St. Thomas Christians*. Orientalia Christiana Analecta, no. 241. Rome: Pontifical Oriental Institute, 1992.

Moraes, George Mark, *A History of Christianity in India*. Bombay: Manaktalas, 1964.

Navakatesh, J. Thomas, *Die Syrisch-Orthodoxe Kirche der Südindischen Thomas-Christen: Geschichte, Kirchenverfassung, Lehre*. Das östliche Christentum, n.s., no. 19. Würzburg: Augustinus-Verlag, 1967.

Podipara, Placid J., *The Thomas Christians*. Bombay: St. Paul Publications, and London: Darton, Longman and Todd, 1970.

Tisserant, Eugene, *Eastern Christianity in India: A History of the Syro-Malabar Church from the Earliest Times to the Present Day*. Westminster, Md.: Newman, 1957.

THE ROMAN CATHOLIC CHURCH

The Christian Centuries: A New History of the Catholic Church. Vol. 2, David Knowles with Dimitri Obolensky, *The Middle Ages*. Vol. 5, Roger Aubert et al., *The Church in a Secularised Society*. London: Darton, Longman & Todd; New York/Paramus/Toronto: Paulist Press, 1969, 1978.

Dulles, Avery, *The Catholicity of the Church*. Oxford: Clarendon Press, 1985.

McBrien, Richard P., *Catholicism*. New edition. [San Francisco]: Harper San Francisco, 1994.

McKenzie, John L., *The Roman Catholic Church*. London: Weidenfeld and Nicolson; New York: Holt, Rinehart and Winston, 1969. Doubleday Image Books ed., Garden City, N.Y.: Image Books, 1971.

The New Catholic Encyclopedia. 15 vols. New York: McGraw-Hill, 1967. Reprint + supplementary vols., Palatine, Ill.: Jack Hagerty; Washington: The Catholic University of America, 1981 (vols. 1-17), 1988 (vol. 18).

~

APPENDIX F

Directory of the Roman Catholic Church and the Oriental Orthodox Churches in the United States of America

I. THE ROMAN CATHOLIC CHURCH —————————

Head: His Holiness Pope John Paul II (Vatican City State)

The National Conference of Catholic Bishops
President: Cardinal William Keeler, Archbishop of Baltimore, Maryland

The Standing Committee of Bishops for Ecumenical and Interreligious Affairs
Chairman: Most Rev. Oscar H. Lipscomb, Archbishop of Mobile, Alabama

Secretariat for Ecumenical and Interreligious Affairs
Executive Director: Rev. John F. Hotchkin
National Conference of Catholic Bishops
3211 Fourth Street, N.E., Washington, DC 20017-1194
Tel: (202) 541-3020 Fax: (202) 541-3183

II. THE STANDING CONFERENCE OF ORIENTAL ORTHODOX CHURCHES —————————

1. The Armenian Orthodox Church
Head: His Holiness Karekin I, Supreme Patriarch and Catholicos of All
Armenians (Etchmiadzin, Armenia)

The Eastern Diocese of the Armenian Church in America
Primate: Archbishop Khajag Barsamian
Chancellor: Rev. Garabed Kochakian
Diocese of the Armenian Church of America
630 Second Avenue, New York, NY 10016
Tel: (212) 686-0710 Fax: (212) 779-3558

The Western Diocese of the Armenian Church in America
Primate: Archbishop Vatche Hovsepian
Diocese of the Armenian Church of America

St. Gregory Armenian Church
2215 East Colorado Boulevard, Pasadena, CA 91107
Tel: (818) 683-1197 Fax: (818) 449-7039

2. The Coptic Orthodox Church
Head: His Holiness Shenouda III, Pope and Patriarch of Alexandria (Cairo)

Archdiocese of North America
Primate: Pope Shenouda III

Ecumenical Officer: Rev. Yacob Ghaly
Virgin Mary Coptic Orthodox Church
41 Main Street South, Spring Valley, NY 10977
Tel. and Fax: (914) 356-5257

3. The Ethiopian Orthodox Church
Head: His Holiness Abuna Paulos, Patriarch of the Ethiopian Orthodox Church (Addis Ababa, Ethiopia)

Archdiocese of the United States and Canada
Primate: Archbishop Matthias[1]
P.O. Box 77262, Washington, DC 20013
Tel: (301) 894-2409 Fax: (301) 894-0924

4. The Syrian Orthodox Church
Head: His Holiness Ignatius Zakka I Iwas, Syrian Orthodox Patriarch of Antioch and All the East (Damascus)

The Archdiocese of the Syrian Orthodox Church in the United States and Canada
Primate: Archbishop Mar Athanasius Y. Samuel (died in April 1995)
Ecumenical Officer: Rt. Rev. Chorepiscopus John Meno
49 Kipp Avenue, Lodi, NJ 07644
Tel: (201) 778-0638 Fax: (201) 773-7506

---

[1] Archbishop Matthias's predecessor, Archbishop Yeshaq, broke communion with the Patriarchate in Addis Ababa in 1992. Subsequently he was suspended by the Holy Synod of the Ethiopian Orthodox Church and replaced by Archbishop Matthias. However, Archbishop Yesehaq still holds the allegiance of many Ethiopian Orthodox in this country, and continues to maintain his office at 140-142 West 176th, Bronx, NY 10451. Tel: (212) 299-2741.

The Malankara Archdiocese of the Syrian Orthodox Church in North America[2]
Primate: Metropolitan Mar Nicholovos Zachariah
175 Ninth Avenue, New York, NY 10011
Tel: (212) 337-3450 Fax: (212) 366-6147

Ecumenical Officer: Rev. Paulos Peter
8 Waterford Way, Syosset, NY 11791
Tel: (516) 922-3127

III. OTHER ORIENTAL ORTHODOX CHURCHES

1. The Armenian Orthodox Catholicate of Cilicia
Head: His Holiness Aram I, Catholicos of the Great House of Cilicia
(Antelias, Lebanon)

The Eastern Prelacy of the United States and Canada
Prelate: Archbishop Mesrob Ashjian
Prelacy of the Armenian Church of America
138 East 39th Street, New York, NY 10016-0985
Tel: (212) 689-7810 Fax: (212) 689-7168

The Western Prelacy of the United States
Prelate: Archbishop Datev Sarkissian
Prelacy of the Armenian Church of America
4401 Russell Avenue, Los Angeles, CA 90027
Tel: (213) 663-8273 Fax: (213) 663-0438

2. The Malankara Orthodox Syrian Church of India
Head: Baselius Mar Thoma Matthews II, Catholicos of the East, Catholicos
of the Apostolic Throne of St. Thomas (Kottayam, India)

Archdiocese of North America
Primate: Metropolitan Mathews Mar Barnabas
80-34 Commonwealth Boulevard, Bellerose, NY 11426
Tel: (718) 470-9844 Fax: (718) 470-9219 ∼

---

[2]   The Malankara Syrian Orthodox Church in India is headed by Mor Baselios Paulose II, Catholicos of
the East, and is dependent on the Syrian Orthodox Patriarchate in Damascus. The Archdiocese in
North America depends directly upon the Syrian Patriarch.